Merleau-Ponty
at the Gallery

SUNY series in Contemporary Continental Philosophy

Dennis J. Schmidt, editor

Merleau-Ponty at the Gallery

Questioning Art beyond His Reach

Véronique M. Fóti

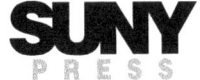

Published by State University of New York Press, Albany

© 2020 State University of New York

All rights reserved

No part of this book may be used or reproduced in any manner whatsoever without written permission. No part of this book may be stored in a retrieval system or transmitted in any form or by any means including electronic, electrostatic, magnetic tape, mechanical, photocopying, recording, or otherwise without the prior permission in writing of the publisher.

For information, contact State University of New York Press, Albany, NY
www.sunypress.edu

Library of Congress Cataloging-in-Publication Data

Name: Fóti, Véronique M., author
Title: Merleau-Ponty at the Gallery: Questioning Art beyond His Reach | Véronique M. Fóti, author.
Description: Albany : State University of New York Press, [2020] | Series: SUNY series in Contemporary Continental Philosophy | Includes bibliographical references and index.
Identifiers: ISBN 9781438478036 (hardcover : alk. paper) | ISBN 9781438478029 (pbk. : alk. paper) | ISBN 9781438478043 (ebook)
Further information is available at the Library of Congress.

10 9 8 7 6 5 4 3 2 1

In memory of
Reiner Schürmann and Louis Comtois

Contents

Acknowledgments		ix
Introduction: A Plethora of Issues		1
Chapter 1	Transcending Profane Vision: The Art of Giorgio Morandi	13
Chapter 2	At Vision's Crossroads: Body, Animality, and Cosmos in the Art of Kiki Smith	27
Chapter 3	Image and Writ in Cy Twombly's Visual Poetics	43
Chapter 4	Resonances of Silence and the Dimension of Color: The Art of Joan Mitchell	61
Chapter 5	Plant Drawing, Abstraction, and the Philosophy of Nature: The Art of Ellsworth Kelly	75
Chapter 6	Strong Beauty and Structures of Exclusion	93
Conclusion	More Ethereal Bodies	107
Notes		113
Selected Bibliography		139
Index of Topics		149
Index of Persons		151

Acknowledgments

When this book was as yet little more than an idea, I visited Kiki Smith's exhibition, *Sojourn*, at the Brooklyn Museum. As it was a day of torrential, wind-driven rain, I gave up on carrying documentation, a notebook, or any purchased materials. Later on I contacted the museum in a quest for information, mentioning my inchoate book project. I received the most gracious and helpful reply from a staff member whose name I have unfortunately lost, but to whom I still wish to express my appreciation.

I also wish to thank Ravi Sharma of Clark University for taking time out from his academic schedule to help me with computer issues involved in getting the manuscript into final form. At Pennsylvania State University, Monique Yaari has extended similar help, as has Dale Silliman, Senior Research Programmer, who walked me long-distance through some thorny computer problems. Finally, yet importantly, I wish to thank Leonard Lawlor, my colleague at Penn State, for his sustained support of my work.

Introduction

A Plethora of Issues

> The transcendence of the thing obliges us to say that it is plenitude only in being inexhaustible, which is to say, in not being fully actual under the look. . . . The senses are apparatus for making concretions in the inexhaustible . . . there is a precipitation or crystallization of the inexhaustible, of the imaginary, of symbolic matrices.
>
> —Maurice Merleau-Ponty, "Transcendence of the Thing and Transcendence of the Phantasm"

Merleau-Ponty's sudden death, in May 1961, not only deprived philosophy of a thinker whose work was incisive and profound as well as wide-ranging in the scope of its intellectual engagements, but it also foreclosed any continuation of his intensive studies of nineteenth- and twentieth-century visual art, and of the challenges it posed to philosophy. Just the summer before his death, he had written *L'œil et l'esprit* ("Eye and Mind") at Le Tholonet in Provence, and he was intensely engaged in writing *The Visible and the Invisible*, now extant only in its fragmentary form. The art that, due to his death, remained immediately beyond Merleau-Ponty's reach was that of roughly the second half of the twentieth century, a century whose artistic innovation and complexity remain, so far, unrivaled. This foreclosure of Merleau-Ponty's own access to recent and contemporary art has given rise to a widespread and somewhat unfortunate tendency among scholarly commentators to focus predominantly on the very same artists or artistic movements with which he himself engaged: prominently Cézanne, followed by Klee, Matisse, Rodin, and the challenges faced and posed by postimpressionism and cubism. His own focus may also have been somewhat culturally restricted, in that he did not consider contemporary movements in Italian art, such as Futurism, *arte povera* (poor art), or *pittura metafisica* (metaphysical painting), nor yet German Expressionism or, finally, the postwar rise and quick ascendancy to international fame of American abstract painting. The scholarly tendency just criticized has further been paired with a proclivity to concentrate on the issues that the philosopher himself discusses in his aesthetic writings, rather than engaging directly with artworks and the practices of artmaking, bringing them into dialogue with Merleau-Ponty's phenomenology.

Fortunately, however, some recent scholarship has, to a significant extent, overcome these scholarly restrictions. In *The Retrieval of the Beautiful: Thinking Through Merleau-Ponty's Aesthetics*, Galen A. Johnson carries out in-depth analyses of Cézanne, Rodin, and Klee, in relation to Merleau-Ponty, linking them critically with a discussion of Barnett Newman's rejection of beauty in favor of sublimity, and further with Jean-François Lyotard's exaltation of the sheer event.[1] In *Art, Language, and Figure in Merleau-Ponty: Excursions in Hyper-Dialectic*,[2] Rajiv Kaushik explores Merleau-Ponty's notion of the "autofigure" in the context of his understanding of a "figured philosophy." He situates Cy Twombly's art (particularly his early "graffiti" pieces) at the site of an intersection between figuration and erasure, and between interiority and exteriority, which he also studies in relation to Klee's graphism. Mauro Carbone, in *The Flesh of Images: Merleau-Ponty between Painting and Cinema*,[3] and in many of his other writings, has investigated the philosophical import of Merleau-Ponty's sustained interest in film. Anna Caterina Dalmasso's recent work, *Le corps, c'est l'écran: La philosophie du visuel de Merleau-Ponty*,[4] offers not only a rich discussion of the philosophy of cinema and of the technologies involved in contemporary visual culture, but also an in-depth analysis of Merleau-Ponty's 1953 lecture course at the Collège de France, "Le monde sensible et le monde de l'expression" (The sensible world and the world of expression),[5] showing that it initiates his late ontology. In 2012, Saara Hacklin defended a doctoral dissertation at the University of Helsinki titled "Divergencies of Perception: The Possibilities of Merleau-Pontian Phenomenology in Analyses of Contemporary Art," in which she focused chiefly on contemporary Finnish artists.[6] Finally, although David Morris's profound and challenging new book, *Merleau-Ponty's Developmental Ontology*,[7] does not directly address Merleau-Ponty's philosophy of art, but rather the emergence of sense or meaning within material and energetic nature itself, it establishes a standard and frame of reference with respect to which phenomenological studies of artistic practices and visuality will need to situate themselves.

Taking part in this scholarly conversation with a clear focus on visual art, this book seeks to interpret the work of a selection of artists in dialogue with Merleau-Ponty's thought. Although these artists (who are American, with the exception of Morandi, but also introduce a more international perspective in that Mitchell and Twombly were expatriates, with Twombly being also a restless and intercontinental traveler) can roughly be dated to the second half of the twentieth century, no exact temporal delimitations can be established. Thus, for instance, Giorgio Morandi (1890–1964) outlived Merleau-Ponty by just three years, but Cy Twombly and Ellsworth Kelly lived and worked into the twenty-first century, and Kiki Smith is a living artist whose future work cannot be foreseen.

Given that no guiding principle of selection interlinks the chosen artists (or, to put it autobiographically, this book took its start from the writer's fascination with certain artistic practices and issues, rather than from a philosophical agenda to which art would be subservient), a measure of heterogeneity prevailed. Heterogeneity is of course a key characteristic of twentieth-century art, and the artists discussed here have often embraced it and integrated it into their work, along with contingency (this is strikingly true of Smith, Twombly, Mitchell, and Kelly). Morris, moreover, points out the radical contingency of philosophy itself, particularly of phenomenology, which, he writes, "can be rigorously empirical only to the degree that it understands its very own concepts and sense as radically contingent on radically contingent being."[8] Nonetheless, to allow heterogeneity and a certain contingency to inform the very structure of a philosophical work is to risk a lack of theoretical coherence that, as the writing of this book took shape, was a concern.

Somewhat surprisingly and utterly refreshingly, however, it quickly became clear that practices of artmaking as heterogeneous as Morandi's still lifes, Smith's complex and sculpturally informed installations, Twombly's graphism, Mitchell's gestural abstraction, or Kelly's plant drawings entered on their own into quasi-dialogical interchanges that were often inspired (though without explicit reference) by Merleau-Ponty's probing analyses of art (thus showing that their relevance extends tacitly far beyond the art that they explicitly address. These interchanges, however, did not simply confirm the philosopher's analyses but also, at times, deepened or complicated them or introduced critical perspectives. This introduction will explore some of these convergences explicitly, so as not to leave them dispersed and partly concealed within the details of the individual chapters.

Interweaving Dualities

Merleau-Ponty's insistence that there is no genuine duality between figuration and abstraction[9] is based not so much on art-theoretical analysis, but rather on his ontological understanding of visuality, or of what Mauro Carbone highlights as the notion of *voyance*, characterizing it as equivalent to the Merleau-Pontyan notion of Flesh, understood as a diacritically differential dynamic involving the expressive reciprocity of seer and seen.[10] There is nowhere within this dynamic any primacy of the supposedly "real," as positively and normatively given, over its expressive configurations (the more so since perception, in Merleau-Ponty's understanding, is already primordially expressive). This dynamic, however, is concealed by ordinary or "profane" vision in its quest for familiarity and identification. This quest is, nonetheless, challenged importantly by the painter's or other visual artist's vision,[11] for which the created image is in no way reproductive or secondary to a pregiven reality.

Morandi and Kelly, in particular, echo and amplify Merleau-Ponty's insights not only in their art, but also in reflective statements. Far from treating everyday objects—the protagonists of his still lifes—as displaying an incontestable and univocal material reality fully offered to sight, Morandi finds their visual presencing to be alien and incomparably surreal. Kelly stresses the need to do justice to "what the eye sees."[12] Doing so, however, does not invite mimetic adequation or reproductive fidelity (which caters only to Merleau-Pontyan "profane vision") but requires, to the contrary, an autonomous visual articulation. To do justice to what is truly seen is to engage with the event of coming to appearance or presencing itself, which everywhere involves the invisibles of the visible and which may, ontologically speaking, preclude the recognition of an ultimate self-withdrawing source akin to Heidegger's Being of beings. To recognize such a source would reaffirm duality (even though Being is always the Being of beings from which it can in no way dissociate itself). It would legitimate the binary and exclusionary conceptuality proper to metaphysical discourse rather than allowing it to be genuinely overcome. In refusing to recognize or to be bound by conventionally recognized as well as ultimate duality, visual art acknowledges the pervasively enigmatic character of presencing or coming to appearance; and it calls it insistently to the viewer's attention.

Materiality is no less enigmatic in its visual presencing than are felt or oneiric qualities, as well as spatiality (or emplacement) conjoined with temporality. It is striking that, for both Morandi and Kelly, forms often tend to become desolidified (and thus, in a conventional sense, dematerialized) in favor of process and of the powers of light. They thus render explicit, in advance of intellectual thematization, their participation in the play and the eventfulness of coming to appearance.

Image and Writ

One conventionally recognized duality is that between image and writing or text, even though, outside the context of Western art, this duality has long, and in various ways, been negated by the arts of Islamic calligraphy as well as of Chinese and Japanese brush writing. In the artistic practice of Cy Twombly, however, replete as it is with erasures, dysgraphy, and pseudo-writing, or in Klee's "pictorial writing," Basquiat's graffitilike inscriptions and near-erasures, or Mark Tobey's "white writing" (which borrows from the Near and Far Eastern calligraphies just mentioned), the image and writ are more often in tension than forming a unitary whole. Whether they foreground their differences through an emphasis on complementarity or on dissonance, neither image nor writ enjoy integrity or purity. The text may in fact be only a semblance or a ghost of writing (a ghost that has long haunted the cultures of the three religions "of the book," Judaism, Christianity, and Islam) by refusing decipherable meaning or by being reduced, by means of erasures, to the status of a trace. Twombly, moreover, subverts the integrity of his text (often taken from lyric poetry) by actively fragmenting and reconfiguring it. Even—or perhaps all the more—when reconfigured, the text contaminates the image and deprives it of any assured self-containment. The artworks thus understood attest to a certain devastation or inability, on their part, to communicate univocally a fully shareable meaning. Meaning instead presents itself as withdrawn into the obliterated past or else as promised and thus future, and therefore as always on the threshold an being interminably withheld. Image and text thus not only call attention to but also complicate Merleau-Ponty's understanding of the invisibles of the visible while also calling into question any straightforward complementarity or harmony between eye and mind. Where inscription, moreover, finds itself reduced to the (scribbled) invocation of mythical or historical ancient names, or to the attributes and associations of ancient Greek, Egyptian, or Roman deities and historical figures (such as Virgil), these names are from the outset placed under the sign of irretrievable loss. The artworks that they inspire hence cannot lay claim to the power ascribed to them by

Heidegger of setting up an exemplary and compelling human historical lifeworld while also setting it back into its tensional relationship or strife against unconstrained presencing or presencing's equally unconstrained, and thus inexplicable, refusal.[13] Artworks can hence neither univocally formulate or interpret, nor yet support, a historical mandate issuing from a quasi-Heideggerian perspective on the "history of Being" (*Seinsgeschichte*). Their reticence and their affinity to the trace carry ethical import through their determined resistance to becoming subservient to ideology, authoritarianism, and totalization.

Artworks and Things

In "The Origin of the Work of Art" (in its final version of 1936), Heidegger poses the question of how to understand the undeniable, if sometimes uncomfortable, kinship between artworks and things. He finds that the humble "mere thing" of nature, such as a block of granite, is characterized by an unconstrained and enigmatic self-containment, or resting-within-itself, whereas the artwork no less enigmatically confronts the viewer with its causally inexplicable and unforeseeable createdness. Notwithstanding its striving to communicate, the artwork is thus more closely akin, for Heidegger, to the mere thing than to the familiar things of use or utensils, even though these, like the work, are humanly created. They are, however, commonly encountered, not in their mysteriousness, but straightforwardly in their serviceability (*Dienlichkeit*), which Heidegger goes on to think at a deeper level as reliability (*Verlässlichkeit*), in that humans can entrust or even abandon themselves to the ways in which things of use configure their lifeworld.[14] He elaborates this by the example of his figure of a Black Forest peasant woman's reliance on the shoes that carry her through her arduous workday, as well as on the ancestral implements that allow her home to be a place of care and nurturance as well as of the events of birth and death. Her implements (probably mostly handmade) are meaningful through their connection with the traditional rhythms of life; but outside of such a connection, things of use for Heidegger degenerate readily into mere usefulness and boring everydayness (to say nothing of sheer detritus or consumer waste, which he does not address).

In contrast to Heidegger's hesitations as to things of use in their ordinariness, together with his contempt for banality, Kiki Smith's art exalts the things of daily use without depriving them of their enigmatic aspects.

She is also sensitive to the fact that, within the historical parameters of women's life situations, their artistic creativity has often expressed itself through craft-based work embellishing things of use. These creations often quite extravagantly imbue home and family life with aesthetic delight and richness of meaning.

Smith also considers the historical implements of daily life (now often collected by museums) to have "memories," and thus to be capable of calling up, and initiating the viewer, into modes of life remote in time, culture, or geography. Since Smith herself is accomplished in a wide range of media, including both electronic and traditional craft techniques, things of use, whether historical or contemporary, often form part of her installations. It is also significant that she associates a meditative dwelling with things of use with offering resistance to the violence pervasive in contemporary culture.

When Heidegger resumes his meditation on things in his essay "Das Ding" (The thing) of 1950,[15] he no longer seeks to set apart simple things of nature from works of art and from things of use, but rather he endeavors to understand the very thing-being of things. Contrary to the ordinary understanding of things as exemplary of solid material reality, he now thinks the thing in terms of its fundamental insubstantiality, in that it configures itself out of emptiness (*die Leere*). The thing is thus deprived of substantive identity and thought rather in relation to the dimensions of the Fourfold of earth, heaven, divinities, and mortals, which it gathers (while nonetheless safeguarding their distances) into the proximity of an event of presencing. The thing thus gathers the free or unconstrained "mirror play," or the "ring" of the Fourfold, into a world that may hold sway, and it brings the world close.

Although Merleau-Ponty does not explicitly address the thing-being of things (nor engage with the echoes of Daoist thought prominent in Heidegger's essay), he grants to things a fundamental insubstantiality in affirming that, being mutable and, in their mutability, inexhaustible, they are never given in full presence or actuality. It is perhaps the nonpositivity of things in their presencing that underlies his rejection, with respect to visual art, of the duality of figuration and abstraction. The work of art, thing though it may be, is privileged in that it not only participates in but reveals and highlights this nonpositivity. The work of the artists discussed here, particularly those of Morandi and Mitchell, attest to their recognition of the nonpositivity of presencing. Although Morandi's art espouses the classical and figurative formats of still life and landscape, it is haunted by the insubstantiality of forms that are, for him, interpenetrated by space, as well as attesting to the plasticity of space and the corrosive powers of light. Mitchell, in her gestural abstraction, is in quest of essentiality and truth while repudiating the classical conception of truth as a conformity of mental representation to commonsensical "reality," and also as capable of linguistic explanation. Art thus shows itself to be more fundamentally attuned, in a challenging way, to the ontological understanding that both Heidegger and Merleau-Ponty seek, in different ways, to develop in their late thought.

The Artist within Her or His Time

In "Eye and Mind," Merleau-Ponty reflects that "the painter is alone in having the right to look at all things without the duty of evaluation."[16] The statement echoes his view, voiced in "Indirect Language and the Voices of Silence," that painting inhabits "a dreaming eternity" detached from knowledge and action.[17] Although in "Eye and Mind" he speaks only about painting's "right" to withdrawal, rather than of its actual or inevitable practice thereof, even this late statement is questionable.[18]

At the time of this writing, visual art is often preoccupied with the issues of colonialism, race, sexuality, gender, and politics; but even in the recent past, when it still cultivated the reticence of minimalism, if not, to use Merleau-Ponty's phrase, ever "since Lascaux," it has engaged with the experience and exigencies of its time. The creation of meditative or contemplative and thus silent work is no less a response by the artist's particular sensibility (formed by factors such as temperament and life history) to the ambitions, exaltations, or traumas of the time. It is thus, as a response, individual and finite and cannot absolutize itself, even though the quest for meaning and the call to responsibility, which it heeds, are not finitized.

Of the artists discussed in this book, Smith and Kelly stand out most clearly for their engagement with aspects of contemporary life, although Twombly's concern with war, vengeance, and violence, approached through ancient Mediterranean history or mythology, must not be marginalized. Smith's focus, in much of her art, is on "being alive here in the body," whether human or animal, and on both the body's expressivity and exposure and vulnerability to trauma and violation. Given her sense of the contemporary urgency of the threat of ecological devastation, her art has also, since the mid-1990s, importantly addressed animal bodies and the human interbeing with animality, and ultimately with the elemental and cosmic dimensions of nature.

Kelly's career-long practice of drawing plant forms from life, as well as making them the basis of lithographic works (and ultimately of his distinctive "way of seeing," whatever the medium) goes beyond human interbeing with animality to reach into the still philosophically neglected understanding of vegetal life's modalities of perception and of world articulation, drawing here on Jakob von Uexküll's pathbreaking researches into the lifeworlds (*Umwelten*) of animals who were, within the parameters of his own research, mostly primitive invertebrates (and thus hardly at a significant remove from plants). Given that von Uexküll's lifework was well known to Heidegger and influenced his conception of human world articulation (that is, of Da-sein's *Umwelt*), one needs to recognize its prefigurations within animality but also to move beyond this zoological focus to recognize the importance of addressing plant-being (concerning which Merleau-Ponty maintains an unbroken silence).

Kelly's devotion, from an early age, to studying the appearance of life forms, such as insects, fish, and importantly birds, together with his almost career-long studies of plants, makes for a practice that served to discourage an understanding of artistic creation in terms of the artist's pure subjectivity, juxtaposed to an objectification of natural life. Objectification encourages uncaring indifference and thus supports ecological devastation, whereas an artist's attentiveness to the aesthetic creativity and refinement of natural life serves to bring home its preciousness and the compelling need to safeguard it.

Notable within the complexities of Kelly's art is, furthermore, his full integration of painting with architecture. In his numerous public commissions, which included a wall of the UNESCO building and the LVMA Forum Auditorium, both in Paris, as well as the Boston panels that transformed a previously dull courthouse into an energized and engaging space full of visual surprises, he realized his ambition of creating large, content-specific public works. The component panels of such works, painted on surfaces such as wood or aluminum, maintain a fine-tuned balance between being integral to the architecture and constituting autonomous works of art.

Before painting came to be understood largely in terms of oil or acrylic discrete works on canvas, it often adorned architectural spaces in the form of murals or frescoes, painted ceilings, or, in more remote times, the painted interiors of the rock-hewn caves of Ajanta, Ellora, or Dunhuang. Painting that is integral to architecture and thus to the configuration of public (or ceremonial) spaces visually and even viscerally communicates the ideas and ideals preeminent in its time. It has the ability to shape the comportment and interrelations of individuals that pass through or linger within these spaces. Painting thus shows itself, as Kelly appreciated, to contribute actively to shaping the public domain as the arena of thought and action.

The Question of Beauty

Merleau-Ponty credits animals with inventing visibles (*inventer du visible*),[19] but they also invent sonorities as well as forms of aesthetic expression that might be likened to dance, choreography, architecture (as in bower birds), or athletic performances that constitute an aesthetic display. In *The Evolution of Beauty*, ornithologist Richard O. Prum defends and further develops Darwin's contested as well as neglected theory, in his *The Descent of Man*, that evolution driven by natural selection is complemented by a drive toward aesthetic pleasure in excess of adaptive advantage.[20] Adolf Portmann already discussed the fact that the elaboration of sheer appearance and display can counteract and compromise utility. Prum's example of such a preeminence of aesthetic desire and delight over survival advantage is that of the male club-winged manakin, a bird that uses its wings for extraordinary musical sound production to the detriment of efficient flight. Due to the peculiarities of avian embryonic development, this detriment also afflicts females (to whom, nonetheless, the performance is offered).

In Prum's view, female mate choice is the impetus for animal (particularly avian) aesthetic creativity and accomplishment. The avian female is an exacting judge of her suitors' appearance and aesthetic achievements, but her species-specific criteria are fundamentally arbitrary rather than embodying ideals of beauty that could be universalized. If aesthetic creativity governs mate choice and thus species survival, Portmann's "unaddressed appearances" (which are elaborated in the absence of any possible eye to appreciate them) point to the excess of aesthetic creativity in organismic nature over utility in any form.[21] Beauty, however it is elaborated, seems to constitute a vital need for organisms ranging from invertebrates, and even primitive microscopic organisms, to higher animals.

The vital importance of beauty renders its eclipse in twentieth- and early twenty-first-century art and art theoretical discourse problematic and challenging. Of the artists discussed in this book, none rejected beauty; but perhaps especially Mitchell and Smith explicitly recognized it. Although Mitchell expressed her fundamental and professed commitment to beauty in the powerful beauty achieved by her best work, such as *To the Harbor-*

master (1957), *Morning* (1971), or, as discussed in chapter 4, her suite of paintings known as *La Grande Vallée* (The Great Valley), her realization of beauty is persistently achieved at an extreme of tension (fundamentally between chaos and order) offering no harmonious resolution. Smith, who also values beauty, finds it chiefly realized in works that have a "cut" in them in that they do not reject, but rather acknowledge and transmute, ugliness. Agnes Martin (discussed briefly in chapter 6), understands beauty as ideal perfection; but perfection for her is essentially insubstantial, lacking plenitude and self-sufficiency. It thus repudiates any effort at dominance or totalization that would validate of hierarchies of perfection. Kelly's art similarly withdraws beauty from what Merleau-Ponty calls positivity by allowing chance at times to complement consummate form.

Such practices of artmaking constitute a salutary response to beauty's trivialization and abuses as well as to its willful withholding. If beauty is indeed a vital need, its abuse as an instrument of domination, or its rejection, are likely to bring about cynicism or desolation. However, much as one may sympathize with Prum's view that there is a need today for "a post-human aesthetic philosophy that places us, and our artworlds, in context with other animals,"[22] one also needs to acknowledge the surpassing, and perhaps unique, importance of the ethical dimension for human life. Art, as a consummate realization of the human quest for meaning and beauty, remains, in its import, indissociable from ethicality, which therefore provides the ultimate context for thinking philosophically about art.

Chapter 1

Transcending Profane Vision

The Art of Giorgio Morandi

Penso que non vi nulla di più surreale e nulla di più astratto del reale.

(I think that there is nothing more surreal or more abstract than the real.)

—Giorgio Morandi

Morandi's well-known statement concerning the surreal and abstract quality of the real as offered to sight[1] is echoed by both Merleau-Ponty (who took no notice of the Bolognese painter whose dates, 1890–1964, mark him as his longer-lived near-contemporary), as well as by Ellsworth Kelly, who has remarked that "if you can turn off your mind and look at things only with your eyes, ultimately everything becomes abstract."[2] Merleau-Ponty argues that there is no meaningful choice to be made between figuration and abstraction;[3] and Kelly's remark even suggests a disjunction between eye and mind for certain painters such as Morandi and Kelly that the philosopher (who placed less emphasis on the bond between eye and hand) would have been unwilling to recognize. Morandi, to be sure, never decisively abandoned figuration and cultivated an engagement with what Paul Auster calls "the wonder of pure thingness."[4] This engagement links his painterly vision to Heidegger's thought concerning the thing in a manner that will shortly need to be explored.

The fundamental sameness (without identity) of figuration and abstraction here shows itself to hinge on an artist's ability to neutralize ordinary or, as Merleau-Ponty calls it, "profane" vision, akin to what Morandi speaks of as the "conventional images" that alienate vision from reality.[5] Whatever the pictorial mode an artist may work in, her inactivation of profane vision is indispensable to the artistic validity of her work. She must therefore decisively reject any understanding of the image as a mimetic representation, or as a secondary artifice standing in for an absent original. In this sense, the image intimates the strangeness of reality as visually apprehended, which then does not conform to the Platonic schema of a nonsensible *eidos* or form that could only be imperfectly approximated by visual (re-)presentation. Taking up Merleau-Ponty's understanding of vision as involving the mutual precession of what is upon the seer, and of the seer upon what is, Mauro Carbone traces out the spatiotemporal dynamics of this double precession without absolute precedence that constitutes the matrix of any artistically relevant visual image.[6] In this sense (and echoing the phrasing of Paul Klee), the image *renders visible* what could not otherwise be so. It is thus hardly surprising that Morandi, who habitually rejected comparisons of his art to that of nonfigurative painters such as Mondrian, could nevertheless tell Janet Abramovicz in 1955 that, had he been born some twenty years later, he might well have become an abstract painter.[7]

The Humble Thing in Focus

Notwithstanding some early portraits and self-portraits, as well as early engagements with cubism and Italian futurism and, from 1916 to 1920, a significant involvement with the movement known as *pittura metafisica* (metaphysical painting),[8] Morandi's work focused chiefly on the still life, complemented by landscape and, in a minor mode, by floral compositions. His still lifes were composed of humble everyday objects such as bottles, canisters, pitchers, or vases, of no particular aesthetic distinction—so that, as recounted by Siri Hustvedt, an exasperated viewer could find only yet "more bottles" in even the last room of a Morandi exhibition.[9] His art, which comprises the media of drawing and etching as well as oil painting, engages with the sheer thingness of things. These things are not, however, the "mere things" (*blosse Dinge*) of nature, to which Heidegger ascribes an enigmatic self-containment shared by works of art in their unconstrained presencing.[10] Morandi's things, in contrast, are mostly things of use (what Heidegger calls *Zeug*); but they are alienated from any context of use without being, for all that, reduced to pure plastic values or forms, so that their function would become a mere pretext for purely formal concerns. Rather, the memory of use and of everyday habituality resonates in them indelibly but without prosaic literality. They remain suspended between the familiar and the strange, or the essentially unknowable that Heidegger likes to call the "uncanny."

In Heidegger's 1950 essay "Das Ding" (The thing),[11] enigmatic self-containment is no longer ascribed solely to "mere things," which repudiate human meaning, or to the irruptive presencing of the work of art, but rather and even in the first place to the humble things of everyday use, such as jar, mirror, or brooch, and ultimately also to both the nonliving and living "things" of nature (Heidegger names, for instance, mountain and stream, and heron or deer).[12] Far from retreating into inaccessibility, the thing is also what remains at issue, in that it concerns and engages humans in their daily lives.[13] What is here in focus is not paradigmatically some object that can be represented (*vorgestellt*) or fabricated (*hergestellt*) in accordance with the Platonic schema of production (*poiēsis*) governed by the Form (*eidos, idea*). Rather, the thing brings close (*nähert*) world, a mutable concept in Heidegger's trajectory of thought, but which is now thought as the onefold and simple (*einfältiges*) gathering together of the Fourfold of earth, sky, divinities, and mortals into the mutuality of their mirror-play. In this play or round-dance (*Reigen*), each of the Four comes eventfully into its own (*ereignet sich*) only by a movement of self-disowning (*ent-eignen, vereignen*) in favor of the "ring" of their mutuality: "The round-dance (*Reigen*) is the ring that rings in that it plays as mirroring. Enowning, it lights up [*lichtet*] the Four into the luster [*Glanz*] of their simplicity [*Einfalt*]. In becoming lustrous [*erglänzend*], the ring dis-owns [*vereignet*] the Four, open to everywhere, into the enigma of their essentiality [*Wesen*]."[14]

In this mirror-play, there is nowhere any insistence on a stable, inherent, or graspable ownness or identity. Thus the "ringing" of the Four, and the thing that grants it a while of appearance, are also *ring* (understood in Heidegger's *Allemannisch* dialect as *gering*) in the sense of being humble, slight, self-accommodating, and easeful. The thing is ultimately of concern to mortals because it can initiate them into what, as mortals, they are uniquely capable of: being toward death, so that they uniquely have access to: "the shrine of nothingness that is the mountain-shelter [*Gebirg*] of being."[15]

Seeking in the three textual versions of Heidegger's "The Origin of the Work of Art" the traces of the acknowledged "turn" (*Kehre*) in his thought that he himself said was connected with this essay, Jacques Taminiaux finds that only the final version of 1936 abandons the tone of "voluntarist proclamation" that characterizes its predecessors.[16] Moreover, as Taminiaux points out, this version is significant due to the fact that "Heidegger's previous contempt for everydayness and its pettiness has now almost vanished . . . [and]

that the first third of the final version is devoted simply to the question, What is a thing in its thingly character?"[17] The change is not only of tone, but of philosophical orientation, and it becomes consummate in Heidegger's 1950 meditation on the thing and on the profound import of its humble status and its seeming insignificance.

Merleau-Ponty may well have been unfamiliar with "Das Ding" (first published in 1951), and the ontological import of everyday things is not among his philosophical preoccupations; but there are formulations in his late ontology, particularly in the Working Notes to *The Visible and the Invisible*, which have a certain kinship with Heidegger's meditation. Thus, in a Working Note of November 1959, he enjoins himself to say that things "are not spread out before us like perspectival spectacles," but that they are, rather, "structures, membranes, the stars of our life" gravitating around us.[18] In a note of May 1959, he reflects that the thing's transcendence (of perceptual apprehension) means that its plenitude is inexhaustible and thus irremediably incomplete or lacunary."[19] The silent persuasion of the sensible thing, he notes in a Working Note of October 27, 1959, "is the only means for being to manifest itself without becoming positivity."[20]

In Morandi's art, things constellate and configure themselves in space out of a luminosity that is at once both soft and radiant and that, in allowing things to become manifest, also veils them and creates ambiguities. It often calls for a rich and subtle palette of grayed earth tones, siennas, golds, and whites, or earth greens and muted violets. This palette is restrained, with a somewhat melancholy echo of classical antiquity; but it is also responsive to Cézanne's chromatic researches, which are integral, for Merleau-Ponty, to instigating the "profound discordance" he experiences in confronting "the universe of classical thought with the researches of modern painting."[21] There is a need then to explore these painterly interrogations of visuality, dissociated as they are from both prosaic literality and from reference to any literary or ideological dimension. They are thus dissociated partly by virtue of their focus on things too humble even to invite identification, or for this study to address the interrelation between Morandi's art and Merleau-Ponty's thought.

Vision, Memory, and Perceptual Nonresolution

As Morandi observed in a 1959 interview, his work concentrated on so narrow a range of subject matter as to incur the risk of boring repetition.

He notes that he neutralized this risk by composing each painting or graphic work as a unique take or variation on a familiar theme.[22]

These variations are attentive to what Merleau-Ponty calls "the imaginary texture of the real," in the context of exploring idealities indissociable from their carnal presencing.[23] They also concern, however, the lucid articulations of form in space, the interrelations of volumes and voids, and the subtle modulations of light, shade, and chromas. These painterly concerns unhinge things and their configurations from customary identification without, however, treating them as mere pretexts for painterly innovation or bravura. The familiar identities of things are not abolished by such a practice of painterly *epokhē*; but rather, they continue to play a part in the articulations of their imaginary texture. Sameness thus never becomes identity, and repetition does not deaden the viewer's involvement and fascination.

It is in fact impossible, as Merleau-Ponty notes, to see things "all naked," as Descartes longed unerotically to see (or rather to think) his piece of wax. Even a simple visual quale (a so-called sense datum) presents itself as a temporally distended crystallization of visibility, "a certain intrication in the woof of the simultaneous and the successive."[24] Rather than seeking to strip things of such accretions, the look envelops them and veils them "with its own flesh," without thereby degrading their sovereign being.[25] What allows for this seemingly paradoxical situation is that vision takes place, not with Cartesian detachment in a straightforward subject-object relation, but in an indissociable interrelation with both sensuousness and invisibles, so that no term of this interrelation has priority. In Merleau-Ponty's phrasing, using the terminology of flesh: "The density of flesh between seer and thing is constitutive, as to the thing, of its visibility, and as to the seer, of his corporality . . . it is the means of their communication."[26]

If even the visual quale, interrogated by the look, interlaces not only seer and seen but also the simultaneous and the successive; the temporal dimension is indissociable from painting (often misconstrued as a purely spatial art). It is then not merely a question of understanding how the intrinsically static arts of sculpture or painting can convey the temporality of motion—a question that preoccupies Merleau-Ponty in dialogue with Rodin. In this dialogue, his focus is on conveying the temporality of motion by showing bodies in positions that are incompossible in simultaneity. His focus expands to address how what is perceptually given is always already subtended by memory, whether cultural, historical, or personal, explicit or latent. A painting, moreover, constitutes a visual concretion of its own process that, for Morandi, was a process of looking intently, over a lifetime, not only at the painting in progress but also at how familiar things continuously present new aspects of themselves in novel conjunctions and in cadences of light. Sometimes not even the look, but only the mere memory of objects is distilled into light or into sparse fragments of their form. Merleau-Ponty does not, however, explicitly thematize: the visual dialogue of the artist with her own work as it takes form, as well as with works of his or hers that have already reached their final state but remain available to inscribe their traces in works yet to come. This visual dialogue probably underlies the searching yet ultimately assured spontaneity, fascinating to Merleau-Ponty, with which painters such as Matisse and perhaps Picasso, shown at work in slow-motion films, placed their next stroke. Siri Hustvedt dwells on Abramovicz's recollection that Morandi, once his works became highly sought after, made collectors wait for their purchases, so that he could carry on a protracted visual meditation on the paintings' past and future interconnections with other works of his, present and past.[27]

Morandi's early *Still Life with Yellow Cloth*, which, as commentators have noted, takes up certain motifs of Chardin's *Le Buffet*, such as a protruding knife and a folded cloth, also contravenes this classical reference by its subtly unfixed perspective.[28] The viewer seems to be looking down on a table draped in white cloth and articulated solely in terms of color; yet surprisingly, the gray metal box with a central light band that rests on it, and that appears in many of Morandi's still lifes, appears to be viewed from a lower vantage point. Within the painting, as a composition based largely on triangles that are articulated in both positive and negative space, three copper objects define themselves as silhouettes within the subtle ambient light, while also catching the light in the form of a slight frontal reflection. The yellow folded cloth both challenges and enhances the still life's muted earth tones, its hue rendered more radiant in relation to the brightest white that surrounds it at the format's far right. It is, however, so precariously placed at the table's edge that it seems to float ethereally in front of it, rather than actually resting on it, thus further enhancing the play of perspective ambiguities.

In the mutual precession of what is there to be seen and of what the painter sees and in her turn offers to sight, silent being, Merleau-Ponty reflects, "comes to manifest its own sense."[29] This mutual precession is in fact vision itself, and it accounts in good part for the centrality of vision's painterly exploration in Merleau-Ponty's ontology. Whereas profane vision does not significantly engage phenomenological exploration, given that it contents itself with identification and subjective valuation, the painter's vision, at its most genuine, enables manifestation to be experienced in its full disconcerting power and strangeness and perhaps also (in contrast to profane vision) in its sacrality. This revelatory power may sometimes bespeak itself, almost paradoxically, in a realist image that in no way baffles identificatory recognition, yet in contrast, it may also call for the pictorial mode of nonfiguration. Morandi's art explores what Merleau-Ponty calls "the imaginary texture of the real," and specifically the "carnal essences"[30] as idealities that remain indissociable from, yet always just at the threshold of, their presencing. This orientation is counterbalanced, however, by Morandi's lucid and purely painterly articulation of form in space, of volumes and voids, and by his subtle modulations of light and chromas. The indebtedness of Morandi's formal lucidity (particularly the clarity of his volumes) and diffuse light to Piero della Francesca has often been noted; and together with Cézanne, Piero remains for him a key inspiration. Merleau-Ponty's carnal essences are themselves characterized by a lucid yet not law-governed cohesion, so that they, like "the moments of the sonata, or the fragments of the luminous field, adhere to one another by a cohesion without concept."[31] They elude one's intellectual grasp; and the memory of sensuous experience that sustains them is not the retention of any content (given that they are "negativity or absence circumscribed"). Merleau-Ponty likens the initiating experience to an initiation that, once accomplished, remains indelible.[32]

Turning to one of Morandi's pencil drawings of a still life dating to 1936[33] (the year that Mussolini solidified his position in Italy by conquering Ethiopia), one faces a far more turbulent dynamic instability than one due chiefly to unfixed perspective or to the autonomous modulations of light and color. While ambiguity as well as turbulence are characteristic of much of Morandi's work from 1929 to 1937, in this exquisitely articulated drawing (for Morandi graphic work was never secondary to painting), contour lines do not, even when emphatic, clearly or univocally define objects. Objects are, moreover, startlingly allowed to interpenetrate one another, or to let intervals of negative space interpenetrate positive forms and call their sovereignty into question. Both form and space are left not clearly definable as such. Light falls where it may without relation to any dominant source or to the perspectival laws of its incidence. The composition is dense and seems to refuse being contained (three of the format's edges truncate the still life arrangement); but far from being chaotic, it is unified by a pervasive and powerful visual rhythm to which forms, values, light, and line are all subordinate. The truncation (not unique to this work) indicates that the rhythm extends beyond the format. Unification, however, does not restore any semblance to familiar reality. To the contrary, it establishes what is shown in a dimension entirely of its own, which one commentator (focusing on another one of Morandi's approximately contemporaneous still lifes) describes as having "the mysterious atmosphere of a spirit world."[34]

Merleau-Ponty considers it to be an "enigma" that vision shows things, "each one in its place," precisely but oxymoronically because they are rivals before one's look, obstructing and eclipsing one another, or that, perhaps more familiarly, perspectival distortions serve to reveal the supposedly true, undistorted shapes of things.[35] He does not, however, fully countenance an art that, like Morandi's, renounces descriptive or identificatory verisimilitude while nonetheless, and consummately, maintaining an entirely classical figurative format, such as the still life or landscape.

In the late 1920s, Morandi explored the landscapes around Bologna and Grizzana in the Emilian Apennines (where in 1959 he and his sisters, with whom he shared the family home on Bologna's Via Fondazza) had a second house built. He did so in a number of etchings that show his mastery of chiaroscuro and that are also replete with descriptive content, such as houses, gardens, fields, or the Savena River. They exhibit, however, what Hustvedt (speaking generally of Morandi's still lifes) calls a quality of alienation that deprives things of "solidity and realness."[36] This defamiliarization allows the images to touch levels of human experience that may be at least partially disconnected from language. It also recalls Merleau-Ponty's reflections, in "Cézanne's Doubt," that Cézanne was in quest of the basis of nonhuman nature on whose tacit support humanity had established itself, so that he exercised a vision "penetrating to the root of things beneath the imposed order of humanity."[37] In Morandi's landscapes, this quality of alienation not only intensified at the beginning of the 1930s but also, in the decade of 1932 to 1942, not only omitted but actively excluded human presence and habitation, with buildings reductively essentialized to geometrical forms (often lacking or only minimally suggesting windows or doors), and the hills, fields, or vegetation forming once again an abstract rhythm.

In the spring of 1943, Morandi was briefly arrested by the Fascist police (OVRA) on suspicion of being involved with anti-Fascist intellectuals and agitators. That summer, he and his sisters indefinitely prolonged their summer retreat at Grizzana in a quest for relative safety, not only from investigation, but also and especially from the Allied bombardment of Bologna. Morandi did not return to the city until December 1944, and, being deprived in Grizzana of his still life paraphernalia, he mostly devoted himself to landscape painting, which he carried on whenever possible *en plein air*. Although some of his landscapes of the early 1940s, which generally show houses against the rise of a hill or glimpsed through tree branches, recall Cézanne's paintings of structures such as the *Maison Maria* or the *Château Noir*, they have none of Cézanne's chromatic vibrancy but focus instead on configurations of architectural shapes and geometric patterns of light and shade in a muted palette. Similarly, while Morandi, like Monet, often worked in series, the seriality of these landscapes does not explore the changes of atmospheric color but rather the subtle variations of vantage point and formal configurations.

Morandi's late landscapes of about 1960 through 1963 radicalize a tendency toward abstraction and minimalist reduction, found already in his landscape paintings of the early 1940s. Architectural forms may now be essentialized as sheer rectangles set within diagonal demarcations that may be starkly geometric or else densely foliar in articulation, as in *Landscape*, 1961.[38] They sometimes show, with particular starkness, the roughly pentagonal forms of two isolated and distant stone houses on a hill in Grizzana, known as the "houses of thirst." In oil, pencil, and watercolor (which, according to Abramovicz, Morandi privileged over etching in his final years[39]), their stark, mostly windowless forms stand out against the rise of the hill demarcating itself against the expanse of the sky.[40] Although Morandi, who considered architecture to be the supreme art, did not relinquish structural clarity, these late landscapes engage once again with perceptual ambiguities (such as those of unfixed perspective), and with the pervasive involvement of memory and imagination in perception, so as to go beyond nature toward an autonomous pictorial articulation that, in its reductive purity, remains powerfully, as well as lyrically, expressive.

Responding to Adversity

As Merleau-Ponty writes in "Man and Adversity," a valuable or great work is never a mere effect of life; but it is rather an unforeseeable *response* "to its very particular happenings or to its most general structures."[41] Morandi lived through two world wars and through the two decades of Italian Fascism; and as an artist, he frequently faced a disparity, beginning in his student days at Bologna's Academia di Belle Arti (Academy of Fine Arts). Having initially been regarded as a star student, he found himself, once he pursued his own vision against the stranglehold of the academy's entrenched conservatism, barely able to pass.[42] Later and sometimes vituperative criticism charged that his devotion to the supposedly minor genre of still life alienated his work from Italy's great humanistic tradition in painting and sculpture, to which the human figure was central. Furthermore, in the prevailing political atmosphere, his engagement with innovative or else "foreign" artistic movements, such as, respectively, Italian futurism or cubism, was considered to compromise the *Italianità* (the essential Italian identity) of his work.

Reflecting on the contemporary experience of prevailing contingency, Merleau-Ponty considers that Fascism is, in important respects, "the shying back of a society before a situation where the contingency of moral and social structures is manifest."[43] As Abramovicz's well-informed research shows, Morandi's relationship to Fascism was complex and ambiguous. Contrary to the biographical "myth" (which he himself supported) of the artist's being utterly apolitical, he did not refuse political involvement by means of a solitary retreat into his painterly absorptions. Although he had no personal affinity to Fascist affirmations, such as those of violence, war, racism, or male chauvinism, he (like many of his contemporaries) treated Fascism initially as a "temporary ally" in a transcendently urgent quest. In his case, the quest centered on the hope that Mussolini's promised "spiritual revolution" would also radically revolutionize the stolid art establishment and give innovative art due scope and recognition. This hope was not entirely unreasonable, given that Italian Fascism, for most of its duration, gave freer rein to the arts than did Nazism and Stalinism).[44]

From 1926 to 1929, Morandi was actively engaged in the Strapaese movement,[45] founded by Mino Maccari and Leo Longanesi, with whom Morandi cultivated a warm and lasting friendship. Although Maccari and Longanesi were outspokenly critical of the regime, they remained committed to Fascism itself, seeking to restore it from within to its supposed "original morality and integrity."[46] Morandi's close connection with this movement eventually enabled him, to quote Abramovicz, "to found his place in the symbiotic web of artistic patronage and favors in Fascist Italy."[47] He was able to secure a position teaching etching at the Academia di Belle Arti and, as a party member (membership being a prerequisite for teaching at a state-sponsored institution such as the academy), he also joined the National Union of Fine Arts and, in particular, its graphic division (Sezione Bianco e Nero), enabling him to exhibit widely. This web of connections eventually served to propel him to a position of international renown. Thus, like some of his friends, he settled into "an ambiguous compromise of adaptation" to Fascism, rather than decisively rejecting it once the hopes that he had initially placed in it were disappointed.

Notwithstanding the meditative silence and iconographic restraint of Morandi's art, it is profoundly expressive and remains responsive to the historical and personal engagements and traumas of his life. Abramovicz comments that Morandi "had no interest in rendering an object's 'reality' . . . he created the still lifes from his mind."[48] She also notes "the haunting introspection and pessimism" that found expression in his art with the decline of the Strapaese movement in 1929, and its founders', Maccari and Longanesi, relocation to Rome.[49] A still life of 1936[50] is painted in close tonal values of muted earth colors such as umbers, grayed ochres, and siennas, together with off-whites. The composition is oriented diagonally, in a falling cadence, and positive or negative spaces are ambiguous or even indiscernible, thus calling into question the ultimacy of the classical figure/ground articulation (to which Merleau-Ponty, given his background in Gestalt theory, remained committed). The 1936 still life's upright forms rise like ghostly apparitions, although at the far right the off-white vase (with a terracotta base) and one of the artist's prized Persian bottles (painted in a roseate earth tone) take on a more defined and assertive stance. Extending diagonally from behind the vase is a scattering of prostrate objects resembling fallen columns, ruins, and bones. Shadows lead their autonomous life; and the one closest to the viewer has the ominous form of a knife.

Abramovicz observes that Morandi's contemporaries failed to understand his still lifes of the 1930s, which, moreover, they had little opportunity to see, given that these paintings were generally edited out of exhibitions.[51] Francesco Arcangeli, his former student as well as his biographer, nevertheless, was alert to the still lifes' being far ahead of their time and anticipating the vision of artists such as Jean Fautrier, Nicolas de Staël, and Wols.[52] Although Merleau-Ponty ignored Morandi, he selected a de Staël painting, *Coin de l'atëlier* (Corner of the studio), for the image file of "Eye and Mind," showing himself to be open to its innovative spirit.

Abramovicz notes that Morandi's palette changed in the 1940s, during the final years of the war, replacing clear, gemlike hues with lugubrious and clouded ones such as purples, mauves, dark crimson, dull yellows, and blackish umbers.[53] Such a palette characterizes a haunting and enigmatic still life of 1942,[54] as to which Pizzetti quotes Morandi's understated comment to his friend Giuseppe Raimondi that "one morning, getting out of bed, this little group of bottles suddenly appeared to me in an uncommon position."[55] Four bottles, the two proximal ones in the shape of pyramids but with their necks bent, and three tall rectangular containers (one with an oval painted on its side) rise from a surface that appears to be tilted forward and whose prominent diagonals (echoed by the open lids of two containers) create a sense of spatial disorientation and are also in tension with the overall prominence of right angles. The long, narrow, nonnaturalistic shadows cast by the containers read as steps leading up to an elevated platform on which the ritual "action" takes place and to which one needs laboriously to ascend. The painting is permeated by a murky illumination, but along the left sides of the bottles there streams a phosphorescent glow. Between and behind the two "pyramids" on the right appear two shapes that cannot be read as still life objects but rather suggest two veiled women, one clearly indicated in a somber hue, with the more distant one barely suggested in a grayed white. Their bent necks are echoed by those of the two pyramidal bottles and by a cork placed askew on the neighboring bottle. Together, these inclinations converge upon the most remote rectangular container that may be read symbolically as a casket. The work's powerful emotional and existential impact shows the anguished experience of a time when, according to Arcangeli, "each individual needed by then to make decisions, alone, about extreme things."[56] It also brings home the realization that not only are figuration and nonfiguration basically equivalent, so that, as Merleau-Ponty writes, vision involves no boundary "defined by the projective visible . . . that painting would have to observe,"[57] and further that, within figuration, the reticent still life is no less capable of expression than is the human figure.

Forms Eroded by Light

In the last eight years or so of Morandi's life, his still life objects or the components of his landscapes are not only configured out of light but are often also eroded and at least partially dematerialized by light. This dematerialization is other than the submersion of forms within light and air that Merleau-Ponty ascribes to impressionism. If, as Abramovicz observes, Morandi "drained his objects of their meaning" and closely approached abstraction,[58] he did so in good part due to understanding light to be the very essence of visible reality, so that solid form reveals their secondary and partly illusional character.

Considering, for instance, a still life in watercolor of 1959,[59] one finds the forms, painted in dark sepia against a pale neutral ground, to be largely unidentifiable. They are touched by illumination, evoked by slivers and specks of the light ground, which allows one to discern a bottle shape on the far left, and perhaps another, barely hinted at, toward the right. Adjacent to these, however, the very ground takes on the form of a bottle, leaving the figure/ground articulation almost undecidable. Ultimately, as Mario Pisini observes, the dominant bottle is defined only "by its absence."[60]

Beginning in late 1958, Morandi initiated a series of drawings and oil paintings showing or suggesting the forms of his two prized Persian bottles; but these tend now to be reduced to rectangular monoliths (even though, in the oil paintings, the paint is used too thinly to suggest stone). The bottle shapes are generally both separated and bound together by dark shadows or else by an intermediary object, which also has become difficult to identify. In two of these still lifes, the intermediary object mysteriously resembles a butterfly with outstretched wings (itself a symbol of metamorphosis). One eventually realizes, however, that it is in fact the truncated and defamiliarized top portion of Morandi's familiar blue-striped bottle. By means of showing the strangeness and instability of forms and their configurations out of light, as well as their erosion by light, Morandi truly shows what Merleau-Ponty speaks of as painting's catching objects "in the act of appearing, organizing themselves before our eyes."[61] However, in this dynamic, Morandi stresses not only emergence and organization, but also dissolution and unstilled mutability.

Looking back to Heidegger's discussion of the forms of things in "Das Ding," one appreciates his realization that, rather than being simply products of manufacture (*Herstellen*), things of use are formed out of emptiness (as is, of course, paradigmatically evident in his favored example of the pitcher). One also appreciates his calling attention to the ensuing donation (*Schenken*), accomplished by the thing's gathering the Fourfold into an event and its granting it a "while" to presencing. Nevertheless, in "The Thing," Heidegger characterizes things, much as he did in "The Origin of the Work of Art," importantly, in terms of their autonomous and stable self-containment. In contrast to the mere object (*Gegenstand*), which literally stands over against (*gegen*) one, the thing is *sebstständig*: it stands autonomously within itself.[62] The genuine thing, for Heidegger, is definitely not mutable nor even possibly eroded by light. It is also not ambiguously encroached upon or interpenetrated by its neighbors, nor is its configuration out of emptiness always on the verge of dissolving again into an empty expanse, as it tends to do in Morandi's late still lifes. Morandi's things exhibit none of the status of Heidegger's as emblems of a traditional mode of life, with a resonance of *Heimat* or of a homeland. Rather, they are truly what Heidegger terms *gering*, namely, humble or insignificant, in that they were gathered largely from household discards or from the random offerings of flea markets. Rather than being evocative of a homeland, they are already and irremediably displaced or discarded.

Morandi's things, as the "protagonists" of his still lifes and landscapes, are not for him akin to how Heidegger thinks of things but rather to how Merleau-Ponty thinks of things in their transcendence. They lack, for him, any reassuring "homeland" familiarity but are, rather, similar to phantasms in being never given fully or in positivity. Since they are, moreover, inexhaustible, they cannot be definitively encompassed by the look that nonetheless seeks indefatigably to espouse them.[63] They do not, to echo Heidegger's phrase, stand independently within themselves (as being *selbtständig*) but are, as already discussed, defined through the mutual precession of vision and visibility. Painting, furthermore, remains wedded to time and change because "it is always within the carnal."[64] To accord autonomous stability to things is still to remain within what Merleau-Ponty terms the framework of classical thought that, as he affirms, the researches of modern painting have profoundly challenged.[65] Philosophy thus still needs to take the full measure of this silent challenge on the part of painting.

Chapter 2

At Vision's Crossroads

Body, Animality, and Cosmos in the Art of Kiki Smith

Toute pensée de nous connue advient à une chair.
(Every thought known to us comes to pass unto a flesh.)

—Maurice Merleau-Ponty

Among the distinctive concerns of Kiki Smith's art, which include her sculptural or graphic investigations of the human body's organic interiority, its vulnerability and proneness to fleshly indignities, as well as the mysterious upsurge of creative inspiration, and the significance of objects of daily use (often created by and important to the lives of women whose creativity has historically been marginalized), this chapter will focus, importantly but not exclusively, on Smith's giving visual presence and power to what Merleau-Ponty speaks of as "the lateral *Ineinander* of humanity and animality."[1] This concern emerges in her art in the mid-1990s, a time when she found that her work no longer followed any straight story line but tended instead to "meander" or enter into "free fall,"[2] and when she turned from a focus on the human, particularly the female body, to nature as a relatively "free space," less encumbered by sociopolitical issues but in need of rethinking in terms of ecological coexistence. Smith's art has further addressed not only the complexities of humanity's inter-being with animality, but also the inter-being of earthly life with elemental nature and with the cosmos.

Modalities of Inter-Being

Human being, Merleau-Ponty affirms in the introductory section of his third lecture course on Nature, needs to be understood in its *Ineinander* or inter-being with animality, and ultimately with the encompassing scope of nature.[3] Smith remarks similarly, if informally and colloquially, that "it is much more beneficial . . . if you align yourself toward coexistence."[4] This implies that, rather than being regarded as the uniquely privileged *zôon logon ekhon*, the living being possessing reason and speech, or else as the supposed "master and possessor of nature," the human being needs first of all to understand itself as "another manner of being a body."[5] In his engagement with Adolf Portmann's studies of animal form in his second Nature course at the Collège de France, Merleau-Ponty affirms that, in higher animals, "the body is entirely a manner of expression."[6] The bodily form or appearance of animals thus cannot be adequately understood as geared primarily to the ends of survival and perpetuation of the species, but rather carries above all "the existential value of manifestation or presentation."[7]

The laterality of inter-being subverts hierarchies or structures of domination; and Smith herself speaks of dismantling "European hierarchical dualism," with its twofold degradation of nature and of women.[8] Merleau-Ponty reflects, in *The Prose of the World*, that it is "the expressive operation of the body, begun already in the least perception," that is carried forward to issue into art. Paleolithic cave painting thus "founded a tradition only because it gleaned from another—that of perception."[9] With respect to paleolithic painting (or sculpture, which was of central importance to the culture, but which he does not discuss), Merleau-Ponty tends to disregard its drawing, not straightforwardly on perception, but also and importantly on a matrix of mythical, ritual, and quasi-magical interpretations of human and animal life, within the context of a cosmic view of life, death, and regeneration (a view that also emphasizes the life-giving creativity of women).This heritage complicates perception, and with it the expressivity of human bodily life, from the outset. Even though it may be largely eclipsed in contemporary globalized culture, it still persists on an oneiric level, as well as within legends or mythic narratives, in the symbolism of iconic characters such as Odysseus or Persephone, and in fairy tales with their play of metamorphosis.[10]

Smith's art draws widely as well as eclectically on myth and fairy tales, investing this immemorial tradition with a new visceral intensity and a gripping visual power. However, whereas a tradition tends essentially to render the lifeworld meaningful, and thus familiar and habitable (even though it acknowledges and safeguards mysteries), her art consistently *defamiliarizes* this heritage, rendering it both enigmatic and disturbing, particularly as concerns the inter-being of animality and humanity. The human figure in her works is predominantly feminine; and this choice of gender gives new complexity and depth to the all-too-familiar association of woman with nature, rendering the association a source not of women's dehumanization but of feminine transformative power. Some of the haunting impact of relevant works derives from Smith's practice of visceral literalization; her art grips and immerses the viewer and does not allow her or him to retreat to the neutralized standpoint of a detached observer or a reflective interpreter—a standpoint that, however, remains implicit in Merleau-Ponty's discussion of animality in the second Nature course.

Birth, often thematized by Merleau-Ponty in its connection with artistic creation, becomes a visceral and enigmatic nexus linking animal and human being in Smith's art. In a life-size bronze, *Rapture*,[11] a mature nude woman, her smooth body gleaming, steps forth from the belly of a wolf lying prostrate on its back as though in both agony and transport. In *Born*,[12] a sculpture of great formal elegance, a mature woman takes birth from a standing doe who gazes back toward her. In the collages titled *Carrier*,[13] a nude woman carries the body of a wolf, either limp and perhaps lifeless or else vigilantly alert, draped across her shoulders. The animal's body is dark and massive, while the woman's (excepting perhaps her dark sex) seems almost to be made of light. The bond of issuance and of "carrying" (with its connotations of pregnancy, so important a metaphor for Merleau-Ponty) and genetic inheritance is also powerfully thematized in *Tied to Her Nature*, in which the slight body of a long-haired girl (similar to Smith's near-contemporary figure of Eve) is roped, in a prone and sexually suggestive position, underneath the belly of a massive ram. The animal gazes with meditative tenderness at her upturned face, while she reaches up delicately to touch the tip of one of its ears.[14] The gestural interchange between woman and animal in these and related works is reticent; and Smith has commented that she prefers implied over explicit gesture or movement.[15]

One of Smith's iconic figures remains the wolf-girl who peers out from a 1999 etching, delicately and demurely dressed, but with her face covered in long, beastly fur.[16] Particularly unsettling is the contemporaneous mixed-media sculpture *Daughter*,[17] which shows a girl, evidently startled at being seen, dressed in a long red cape, the hood of which frames her hirsute face, suggesting to some commentators that she may be born of a union between Little Red Riding Hood and the wolf.[18] However, extreme facial hairiness is in fact a medical condition, known as hypertrichosis, which afflicts the daughters of male carriers; and families menaced by the condition were traditionally shunned as "wolf-people." Another young woman closely associated with a wolf and of particular fascination to Smith is the fifth-century French shepherdess Sainte Geneviève (patron saint of Paris and identified by Smith as the wolf-born woman in *Rapture*[19]), whose radiant kindness pacified a wolf preying on her lambs (a story that prefigures that of Saint Francis of Assisi and the wolf of Gubbio).

Helaine Posner points out that Smith's underlying principle in such works is *contingency*, representing "a temporary coming together of elements rather than an essential or transcendent moment," and citing Smith's conviction that there is *universal mobility*, so that "nothing is fixed."[20] Formally speaking, collage is a medium that works closely with contingency; and Smith comments to Christopher Lyon that she began experimenting with expanding collage into three dimensions but found that the cuts, left visible, became an unwanted focus.[21] More complex efforts at working with the contingencies of cutting and breaking forms and fitting them into new configurations led on to works such as *Sainte Geneviève and the May Wolf*, as well as *Rapture*. Such thematizations of the inter-being of humanity and animality are not, she stresses, "*essential*," and thus fixed and static. She acknowledges, however, that she cannot answer the persistent questions about their meaning, which is not only fluid but also "in some ways . . . very private to me."[22]

Birds, in Smith's art, are figures of spirit, inspiration, or soul, and as such they are, though vivifying, not entirely of this world but possessed rather of enigmatic yet threatened powers. The crow or raven (totemic symbol of the Tlingit nation of coastal North America) appears in a battered state, yet carrying a gold nugget in its beak, in *Black Bird*.[23] In *Head with Bird*, a bird, perhaps a parrot, stands on a severed and upturned human head whose disintegrating features still express agony.[24] In 1995 Smith created several sculptural installations in response to a newspaper report about a flock of crows falling dead from the sky over New Jersey, victims of atmospheric poisoning. *Crows* (or *Six Crows*) shows their stricken bodies spread on the gallery floor; and in *Jersey Crows*, the dead birds are conjoined, in one gallery installation, with an agonized female figure as well as a figure of the prehistoric *Ice Man* on the walls, caught perhaps similarly, and almost timelessly, in mortal fall.[25] Smith has remarked that she had initially (though not as a deliberate, let alone didactic, choice) focused on the body as "the one form we all share," human or animal—a form that makes for vulnerability and exposure rather than self-containment. As Merleau-Ponty reminds his readers, some slight accident of the body suffices to extinguish "the spark of the sentient-sensible" that no mere accident would ever have sufficed to create.[26]

Incarnation

Smith has also linked her focus on bodily form to her Catholic background, noting that "Catholicism is involved in physical manifestations of spiritual conditions."[27] Merleau-Ponty addresses Christianity, and Catholicism (his own religious heritage) in particular, chiefly in two short texts situated near the early and late poles of his philosophical trajectory: "Faith and Good Faith," of 1946, and the sections on "Bergson" and on "Religion" of "In Praise of Philosophy," his 1953 inaugural address at the Collège de France.[28] His stress in these texts is on the Incarnation of Christ as effecting the transition from a purely "interior" religiosity focused on a transcendent God, to a worship of God in history, sociality, and in the quest for justice and mercy. Through the Incarnation, religion becomes "a matter of entering body and soul into an enigmatic life, the obscurities of which cannot be dissipated but can only be concentrated in a few mysteries," so that "spiritual meaning shows itself to be inseparable from its material form" (as indeed it remains for Smith).[29]

In Merleau-Ponty's judgment, Catholicism has tended, however, in its institutional form to "freeze" the transition or interconnection between materiality and spirituality in an unresolved ambiguity and to abort rather than radically to realize the ethical import of the Incarnation. In contrast, Merleau-Ponty points to Bergson's choice to forego his longed-for conversion to Catholicism, in order to remain among those facing persecution in "the fearsome wave of anti-Semitism" that he saw gaining momentum in Europe.[30] It is perhaps not far-fetched—yet hardly remarked upon—that Merleau-Ponty's choice of "flesh" (*la chair*) as an ultimate ontological notion carries a pronounced resonance of the Incarnation and its ethical import. The lecture courses on Nature further prepare the ground for the realization that, if indeed "our relationship to the true passes through others,"[31] these others must include animals (and perhaps also other life forms), along with what is (still in an anthropocentric vein) called the "environment" but is ultimately the cosmic dimension.

Smith, who lives and creates (as Merleau-Ponty did not) in a time of widely recognized ecological crisis, recounts being enjoined in a dream to create a Noah's ark of singular animals.[32] What such a work would really bring home is that even a conventional and seemingly salvific Noah's ark could not hold out any hope for the survival of species reduced to no more than single mated pairs stranded upon a devastated earth. Smith's art, which is characteristically poetic rather than didactic, does not show animals rendered extinct by human agency (as John Prosek's does with respect to the passenger pigeon). She has, however, created some haunting installations, such as the 1998 *Night*, shown at the Hirshhorn Museum and Sculpture Garden, in Washington, DC, and its complement, *Invention/Intervention*, shown at Pittsburgh's Carnegie Museum. In *Night*, four plinths, arranged in rows in a darkened space, hold sculptures of nocturnal animals and other natural forms, mostly in black, and are set over against a black, mural-size photo-etching of Smith's iconic animals: wolf, deer, and bird (peacock).[33] White, the achromatic color opposite to black, prevails in *Invention/Intervention*, which likewise includes both sculptural and graphic components. The animals represented in both installations are modeled on taxidermic specimens in museum collections and so are dead, being artfully preserved and held in memory.

Smith's is thus what Warner calls a "mortal art" embracing bodily life not only in its vulnerability or proneness to violation, but also in its organismic functions, normally hidden from sight, and even in its abjection, recognizing no division between what is supposedly pure or impure. According to Portmann, the organic interiority of animal (and human) bodies is not the locus of their visual creativity, nor even of the bilateral symmetry characteristic of higher animals, which is aesthetically pleasing.[34] Linda Nochlin points to the contrast between Smith's engagement with bodily degradation and the dominant emphasis, within classical and post-classical art, on the (culturally understood) body's sovereign self-containment, even when it is shown in the grip of trauma and extreme pain, as in martyrdom. One can, however, extend the contrast further to note that where art, classical or contemporary, as in the works of Goya or Francis Bacon, does show the body's violation and abjection, it does so with an incisive and brutal harshness that is absent in Smith's work; her "mortal art" embraces and welcomes death no less than life as integral to the incarnate condition. Her empathy is sometimes poignant, as in *Pietà*, a lithograph showing five images of her own seated figure holding her dead cat, Ginzer, whose limbs are gradually stiffening into rigor mortis.[35] She shows herself just *sitting with* the dead animal (rather than overtly sorrowing) in what is another, and fundamental, expression of inter-being.

It is striking, in this context, that Smith draws a connection between one of her most harrowing and hard to see works—with a history of being critically derided—namely, her 1992 sculpture *Tale*,[36] as well as with her later (2002) sculpture *Born*, with its seemingly more affirmative imagery of birth and inter-being. *Tale* shows a woman crawling abjectly on hands and knees, her soiled buttocks leaving behind her an almost impossibly long train, tail, or tale of excrement. Whatever may have been Smith's intentions in creating this work, and although Posner is certainly right in noting that works such as this one come from "a much deeper place" than treating the female body as "the battleground" for sociopolitical issues,[37] *Tale* nonetheless renders graphic the tale of the bodily degradation suffered by the victims not only of AIDS (to which one of her sisters, Beatrice or Bebe, succumbed), but also of toxic shock syndrome. Smith, nonetheless, points out her concern with the ultimately formal issue concerning the self-identity of the body, and of what may, surprisingly, issue from it; and she notes the joint importance to her of formal issues and of issues fraught with "a personal stake."[38]

Play, Beauty

The brain-damaged patient Schneider, whose pathology Merleau-Ponty discusses extensively in *Phenomenology of Perception*, cannot, he notes, respond inventively or creatively to any situation encountered because "he is incapable of playing."[39] He thus can in no way creatively transcend his already impoverished take on present actuality. It is the freedom of play that can allow for transcendence and that also saves art from becoming a sterile oscillation between what Warner calls quickening and petrification, in that it can create and preserve a semblance of life, but only at the cost of stilling and mortifying it.[40] Life, Warner writes, "is mutable and evanescent; it is only nonlife and nonbeing that partake of the immutable character of the work of art."[41] Its character of play, nonetheless, infuses art with the unforeseeability and mutability of life, thus counteracting the Medusa effect (which is at work in techniques such as taxidermy). The work of art, moreover, is far from immutable in that, as Merleau-Ponty stresses, it is possessed of hermeneutic fecundity, as it continues to be encountered and reinterpreted: "It is the work itself which has opened up the field from whence it appears in another light. . . . the power or the generativity of works exceeds any positive relation of causality or filiation."[42]

Whereas in organismic development the whole to be realized informs the development and functioning of parts from the outset, the artwork welcomes contingency (envisaging no ultimate whole), together with its risks and possible ruin to the whole that therefore may or may not ever be realized. The artist plays not only with elements of appearance but also, as Smith emphasizes, with meaning. Furthermore, as noted by her interlocutor, the novelist Lynne Tillman, meaning gets definitively signed over to the play of contingencies once the work is "taken into the culture."[43] At that point, its hermeneutic fecundity becomes utterly unforeseeable and refractory to control.

Play involves a sheer delight in possibilities of invention, in appearance, in skill, as well as often in humor, together with inter-being and, ultimately, as Merleau-Ponty puts it in his second Nature course, and in response to Portmann's researches on animal appearance, in "inventing visibilities" (*inventer du visible*) and thus fundamentally a delight in beauty. Inspired by Portmann's researches, Merleau-Ponty comments that one must seek to grasp the mystery of life "in the way animals show themselves to one another."[44] Given Portmann's contrast between the creativity of animal appearance and the visually uncreative and repetitive interior organization of animal bodies, however, one hesitates to suggest that Smith's early explorations of the organismic interior, or of the biological processes and effluents of the human body, let alone its abjection, can lay any claim to beauty. She reflects that, instead of straightforwardly aiming for beauty, she likes to make figures "that have a cut in them"; and the "cut" attests to the figures' being scarred, mangled, or damaged, and thus alienated from beauty's enticements (even though, one could well argue that such a "cut" is subtly present in the work of classical artists whose achievement of beauty is undisputed, such as many of the Italian Renaissance masters). Smith's resolutely nonbinary thinking embraces the cut and seeks to effract its own way toward a postmodern understanding of beauty as geared no longer to things but rather to the event or the moment of "something happening."[45]

While Smith affirms the importance, to her, of "making things beautiful," beauty for her is clearly not vested primarily in a sheer delight in appearances nor in the interrelations of form, color, and movement in space, a delight that humans share in some ways with a spectrum of animal life. She stresses that beauty, for her, "incorporates the ugliness," thus allowing what is disvalued and rejected to enter into "another space of possibility," beyond exclusionary valuation.[46] Smith does, nonetheless, create works or components of works that are unabashedly beautiful. One may think, for instance, of an exquisite bouquet held by a sculpted slight woman (shown as honored for her performance), and whose white figure is placed against lyrical and enchanting photographs and paintings on glass, or else of artifacts such as *Flower Blanket*, executed as cutwork in Nepalese handmade paper, which formed part of Smith's 2010 installation, *Sojourn*, at the Brooklyn Museum's Elizabeth A. Sackler Center for Feminist Art.[47] The "cut," however, is not absent where beauty becomes compelling; it bespeaks itself rather in an emphasis on transience and contingency, or sometimes in a conjunction of what seems jarringly antithetical, such as the Virgin Mary's serene purity and gesture of mercy conjoined with the traces of appalling violence enacted upon her flesh.[48] Given that Smith's art engages with the ultimate and intercrossed mysteries of birth and death, generativity and mortality, it brings beauty to presence as the depth dimension of flesh, understood in terms of what Merleau-Ponty speaks of as inter-corporeity or inter-animality (which embraces not only human or animal bodily life but even, for Smith, saintly flesh). Smith also speaks of beauty with regard to her work as exercising a certain "benevolence."[49] Her (nonmimetic) cherishing of phenomena, together with the attentiveness that she devotes to creatively and diligently working with them, allows her to bypass hierarchical valuation and thus to let what she engages with become manifest in its (non-univocal) truth.

It is, of course, Heidegger who stresses that truth becomes genuinely manifest when it sets itself into a work (though not uniquely into a work of art): "Appearing [*das Erscheinen*] is," he reflects, "as this being of truth in the work, beauty."[50] For Heidegger, beauty thus understood connotes a dimension of mystery that he thinks of, with respect to the artwork, as the way in which it presents itself in the sheer event and enigma of its presencing, which he terms its createdness (*Geschaffensein*). Createdness is safeguarded or, literally, kept true (*bewahrt*) by those who allow themselves to encounter the work in its unsettling power. The work's createdness thus makes for its enigmatic self-containment, which it shares with "mere things" (such as a rock), but not with humanly made things of use that, Heidegger thinks, are encountered instead in the complex relationships of serviceability or desirability.[51] Given its irruptive character, Heideggerian createdness is alien to the repetitive patterns of everyday life.

Smith's art, in contrast, evokes enigma without distancing itself from daily life and things of use. *Sojourn*, for instance, as installed at the Brooklyn Museum, transgressed the allotted gallery space in that Smith placed ghostly white sculptures, such as figures of women using a spinning wheel or an embroidery frame, into the museum's eighteenth-century period rooms adjacent to the installation. *Sojourn* is inspired by an eighteenth-century American silk needlework image (which is, as such, not alien to the domestic milieu) by Prudence Punderson, titled *The First, Second, and Last Scenes of Mortality* (it was included in the exhibition). *Sojourn* thematizes the mysterious upsurge of inspiration and the urgency of the need to create in women's historically tradition-bound-lives, with their waystations of generativity and mortality. Curator Catherine J. Morris comments that, in *Sojourn*, the Annunciation functions as a metaphor for the enigmatic advent of inspiration.[52] Siri Hustvedt, in her meditative study of Vermeer's *Woman with a Pearl Necklace*, shows that the gesture of Vermeer's woman—her delicately raised hands held in front of her torso and close to her face—belongs to the iconography of Italian and Flemish paintings of the Annunciation contemporary with Vermeer.[53] Although there obviously is, in *Sojourn*, no angel, Smith shows a spirit-bird swooping down, or sometimes enmeshed in a maze, or perched on a nude woman's head.

For Smith, creative work in all its forms extends into the remote past and the veiled future, and thus into the mysterious essence of time. She has remarked that to sculpt figures is to create bodies that spirits may enter or occupy, or "that have their own souls, presence, and physical space."[54] Similarly, she comments that there is a "supernaturalness" to objects, so that objects have memories, and that she looks at them in museums in quest of deep memories and other lifetimes.[55] By the very nature of her understanding of use, objects as things of use are not, for her, as they are for Heidegger, prone to degenerate readily into boring triviality.

In more recent work, such as *Homespun Tales* at the Fondazione Querini Stampalia in Venice, which was installed on the third floor of a *palazzo* housing a collection of porcelains and paintings of domestic scenes by Piero Longhi (1702–1785), Smith draws extensively on early American domestic environments, replete with period American household goods, yet rendering them peopled by women and children based incongruously on Longhi's figures. She comments to Tillman that she found herself attracted to the borderlines of sentimentality as constituting yet another "maligned territory" and as a possible antidote to the contemporary American culture of violence.[56] This aspect of her sensibility contrasts sharply with the removal from ordinariness and domesticity that Heidegger considers to be indispensable to "great" art. Although one might think that Heidegger's reattribution of van Gogh's shoes to a German peasant woman amounts, perhaps, to a vindication of ordinariness, it exemplifies, rather, the contrast he seeks to draw between a tradition-bound meaningful purity and simplicity of life (closely connected to his problematic notion of *Heimat* or homeland), and the leveling and homogenizing effects of technicity or, as he later calls it, the Enframing (*Ge-stell*).[57]

Hermann Schmitz traces in Heidegger's thought from *Being and Time* to the early 1930s the double motifs of breaking with the triviality and "boredom" of everyday existence in favor of a single exalted moment of realization, and of a new understanding of truth as being essentially unconcealment, or as what Schmitz terms *Plakat-Wahrheit* or "poster-truth," linking both of these motifs (in ways too complex to be detailed here) to the philosopher's engagement with National Socialism and his transient exaltation of the person of Hitler.[58] Schmitz notes that truth as emblematic unconcealment is spelled out specifically in "The Origin of the Work of Art" with respect to how a Greek temple can supposedly render manifest what essentially guides a historical people's self-understanding and action.[59] It functions thus within the structure of Heidegger's history of being (*Seinsgeschichte*), rather than constituting a genuine engagement with ordinary life. As concerns his interpretation of a Van Gogh painting of shoes, moreover, neither the real, and very different, lives of aristocratic women in eighteenth-century Venice nor of colonial American women in New England can in any way replicate or even meaningfully relate to the life of Heidegger's imaginary and emblematic Black Forest peasant woman. Not only does domestic ordinariness remain, for him, excluded from the outset from "great" art, but so, in contrast to the artists discussed earlier (who did not thematize art's greatness), does everyday human interchange. As he puts it starkly:

> The more solitary the work, set firmly into its *Gestalt*, stands within itself [and] the more purely it seems to dissolve all relationships to humans, the more simply the thrust [*der Stoss*] that such a work *is* enters into openness [*das Offene*], [and] the more essentially the uncanny [*das Ungeheure*] is thrust open, and what until now seemed familiar [*geheuer*] is overthrown.[60]

If the artwork, in what Heidegger considers to be its essential solitude, dissolves human relationships, it also leaves scant room for play and thus for the inter-being of humanity and animality. As concerns animals, Heidegger denies them, in his 1929–1930 lecture course, *The Fundamental Concepts of Metaphysics: World, Finitude, Solitude*,[61] any access to a genuine environing world (*Umwelt*), such as the biologist Jakob von Uexküll (whose challenging work Heidegger acknowledges) had attributed to them.[62] Where animals are concerned, Heidegger recognizes only an environing ring (*Umring*) of drives that may be "dis-inhibited" or, as it were, unleashed, rather than any genuine *Umwelt* (which he reserves for *Da-sein* alone). His *Umring* transforms animal environments with their inchoate world articulations into prisons rather than acknowledging them to be disclosive openings. In contrast, Merleau-Ponty (who had no known access to Heidegger's 1929–1930 lecture course) allows to animals genuine world articulations and recognizes that these constitute a preculture and that they allow throughout much of their range for sociality and play. These factors are no less fully, if tacitly, recognized in Smith's art as they are theoretically explored by Merleau-Ponty, in dialogue with Uexküll, Portmann, and Konrad Lorenz.

To consider here only one of Smith's relevant works: her *White Mice with Ruby Eyes*[63] shows a large gathering of these small rodents that, along with rats and fruit flies, have been called the pets of science (although they are far from being cherished like pets for their playfulness, responsiveness to humans, or for the simple joy of their bodily inter-being) Smith's installation shows a large number of these mice in a set of characteristic poses, and she interlinks them by the playful arabesque patterns of their tails. One may recall here biologist's David George Haskell's description of another rodent scene, involving gray squirrels convivially enjoying one another's company in a patch of sunlight in the treetops on a winter's day. The animals, he notes, "feel . . . they are our cousins, with the shared experience that kinship implies."[64] The preciousness of bonds of kinship may be subtly expressed by Smith's choice of rubies (rather than colored glass) for her mice's eyes.

Flesh, Continuity, and Event

Reflecting on the contemporary art-theoretical relationship between the beautiful and the sublime, Galen A. Johnson takes up Merleau-Ponty's trope of "laceworks" to characterize continuities that admit, or are ultimately dependent upon, discontinuities such as gaps or hollows.[65] He notes that, whereas Kantian sublimity is evoked by the vastness and power of nature but is alien to art, Merleau-Ponty interlaces nature and perception with history and culture, recognizing only "*differentiation* of one sole and massive adhesion to being which is the flesh."[66] In dialogue with François Lyotard, moreover, Johnson explores the sublimity of the "now" or of the irruptive event. He notes that "the modernist natural sublime is still about the thing;

the contemporary postmodern sublime is about the event, the moment of something happening."[67]

Although Smith works in many of the formats that Johnson considers to be in tune with a focus on the event, including installation, photography, film, and video, thus echoing Johnson's suspicions as to "the category of continuity," there remains a certain emphasis on continuity in her work. The continuity is fundamentally that of "being alive here in the body,"[68] which, for Merleau-Ponty, laterally interlinks humanity with animality, as well as with life and flesh as a whole. This continuity is somewhat in tension with his own emphasis on birth, which is attuned to the sheer event, in that birth represents a personal past that was never present and that remains unavailable to oneself, so that it cannot be appropriated, and also in that it marks, despite its novelty, a poignant repetition in difference of immemorial pasts. The expressive metamorphosis that art accomplishes with the stuff of life thus not only involves the sheer event but also springs from a donation that is prepersonal, issuing from the fundamental and continuous expressivity of flesh. This continuity is in no way positive; and Smith's art highlights its nonpositivity in that, as Tillman remarks, it engages with physicality or the body while remaining resolutely "anti-realistic and anti-naturalistic" in its play with meaning and form.[69] Smith stresses that this play is not gratuitous for her but has instead an inherent necessity, in that it springs from the depths of her own being: "Even if [my art] makes me uncomfortable. Even if I would like to be a totally different artist, different from what I am, at the same time, I know that this is what I have been given."[70]

In keeping with the metaphor of lacework, one might characterize the continuity involved as diacritical, in that meaning emerges (already at the level of perception and bodily experience) out of a differential texture, and thus of interstices and divergences.[71] Richard Kearney, explicating Merleau-Ponty's understanding of the issuance of sense from the intercrossings of diacritical expression with the experience of flesh, stresses that the diacritical formalism of both Saussurean linguistics and deconstruction is alien to Merleau-Ponty, who deploys sign-structures across "incarnational presences" as well as in quest of creative accomplishment. Such accomplishment interlinks the "virtual" dimension of fleshly experience, which must ever again be reconfigured and reimagined, given the inexhaustibility of flesh that remains in excess of any configuration. He finds that the "hospitable reciprocity" between these poles, or between "past and future, event and advent, the lived and the virtual," is spelled out uniquely in Merleau-Ponty's thought.[72] It is, however, also concretely enacted in Smith's art.

For Smith, for whom the mysterious advent of creative inspiration is an abiding theme, the continuities of creative work extend into the remote past and the veiled future, in keeping with Merleau-Ponty's notion of institution. Institution operates here not only at the level of history or of the psychic dimension, but even at the level of material objects, where it makes for the "memories" that Smith attributes to objects of everyday use. This reach into ordinary materiality both extends and complicates Merleau-Ponty's understanding of "the bond between idea and flesh, of the visible and the interior armature that it both manifests and conceals."[73] As he notes in a Proustian vein, a vast range of idealities remain indissociable from their embodiment, so that they derive their fascination from being situated "in transparency behind the sensible, or at its heart."[74] By virtue of presencing in translucency (perhaps a more adequate term than straightforward transparency) within the sensible, such idealities remain "without concept." They are not graspable and thus cannot be possessed, but rather they "possess us." Their power derives from the differential (rather than positive) character of their presencing, and from their unstilled deferral of actual presence.

Since flesh involves materiality, the juncture of idea and flesh invites a further reflection on the materiality of Smith's art, which embraces both contemporary technology and traditional craft techniques, of which Smith is a master. She does not recognize the scission between craft, or "applied" versus "fine" art, entrenched in the Western aesthetic tradition (a scission presupposed by Heidegger's notion of the exclusive relevance, already noted, of "great" art). As Engberg writes, Smith marginalizes no medium.[75] In a manner reminiscent of the work of Eva Hesse, she also accepts and espouses the fragility or impermanence of some of these media. In this connection, but with particular relevance to "modern" (or twentieth-century) painting, Merleau-Ponty reflects on multiplying "the systems of equivalences, [breaking] their adherence to the envelope: of things, which may require one to create new materials or new modalities of expression, but which may also come about sometimes by a re-examination or re-investment of those that already exist."[76] Smith's art practices both forms of innovation, in that her inventive use of new materials and techniques also reinvests traditional registers of painterly or sculptural expression (among which Merleau-Ponty explores in particular line, color, and motion). To mention just one example: In *Revelation*, a dense arrangement of (scripted) strips of handmade Nepalese paper forms both a linear articulation and a volumetric oval enclosure for a prostrate female figure, allowing line to enter upon a new expressive modality.[77]

Although Merleau-Ponty speaks of the elementality of flesh, he does not develop or concretize his understanding of elementality beyond pointing to the ancient (Presocratic) provenance of the notion. Smith's art allows the elements to come to presence, not primarily in their overpowering aspect—such as cataclysmic storms, floods or tsunamis, or ravaging fires, but often in their everyday and easily overlooked modalities of presencing. Thus, for instance, *Dewbow* takes the form of an accumulation of greatly enlarged water drops, suggesting both dew and tears, on the gallery floor. The glass of their facture also dazzlingly refracts the hues of the spectrum.[78]

Smith tends to conjoin the elemental with the cosmic dimension of heavenly bodies (often imagined, in her work, in the complex geometries of star shapes). Stars, in turn, may be conjoined with writhing worms or bronze scat, as in *Paradise Cage*.[79] The cosmic, elemental, or celestial dimensions do not negate or even leave behind the mundane and terrestrial.

Although Smith's art may express (but never didactically advocate) her ecological, feminist, and political concerns, it retains an elusive and enigmatic edge that renders it fresh as well as compelling. Merleau-Ponty's reflections on the inter-involvement of visuality with invisibles "occultly apperceived" and on art's reawakening, within ordinary or "profane" vision, "a secret of pre-existence,"[80] allow one to appreciate this enigma as essential to art (without resorting to an overarching schema such as Heidegger's *Seinsgeschichte* or history of being, and ultimately to realize that, as Merleau-Ponty puts it, "vision is the encounter, as though at a crossroads, of all aspects of Being."[81] The crossroads have long been sacred to Hecate's chthonic powers and are, as such, refractory to univocal articulation.

Chapter 3

Image and Writ in Cy Twombly's Visual Poetics

> It is only when the thought of expression turns into a phenomenology of painting that it reaches the point where it can understand the insertion of expression into the world, and consequently grasp the being of the world as the veiling of sense, as wild *logos*.
>
> —Renaud Barbaras, *The Being of Phenomenon: Merleau-Ponty's Ontology*

In "Eye and Mind," the last text that Merleau-Ponty published during his lifetime,[1] he privileged painting as the art that uniquely draws upon "the fabric of brute meaning of which activism or operationalism," characteristic, in his view, of certain strands of mid-twentieth-century scientific thinking, "does not want to know anything."[2] Painting therefore offers, in his view, and more so than other arts, phenomenological access to "wild being," preparing thus for the ontology that he strove to articulate in his late work *The Visible and the Invisible* (published posthumously as a fragment). Painting, he argues in the opening pages of "Eye and Mind," can lay claim to this privilege precisely on account of its alienation from language, or its silence (which historically was long understood as a handicap, threatening to reduce it to a mere craft or manual expertise), as compared to the recognized and esteemed intellectual and ethical responsibilities of the literary writer or the philosopher. Painting's silence, he finds, allows it genuinely and uniquely *to look* at things without being called upon to offer interpretation, appraisal, or advice.[3]

This late perspective, however, does not define the entirety of Merleau-Ponty's thought concerning the relation between the visual and verbal arts, which remained for him persistently at issue. In "Indirect Language and the Voices of Silence" of 1952, for instance,[4] he criticizes painting's supposed tendency to cultivate a timeless meditation, whereas literature, renouncing "the pleasures of an anachronism," reveals and confronts the actuality of its time.[5] In his 1960–1961 course at the Collège de France, *L'ontologie cartésienne et l'ontologie d'aujourd'hui*, he moves from a critical reading of Descartes's *Optics* (a text discussed extensively in part 3 of "Eye and Mind") to seek in language or speech (*la parole*) "a transcendence of the same type" as the one that he had pointed to in vision.[6] He finds this transcendence to be adumbrated rather than fully realized by visual art.[7] Thus he points out that, whereas Leonardo da Vinci "defends *voyance* against poetry," the literary "moderns" (presumably the nineteenth- and twentieth-century French writers with whom he habitually engages) "outdo him by making of poetry a *voyance* as well."[8] Notwithstanding the intricacies and complexities of the interrelations between the visual and verbal arts as he explores them, however, he calls into question their separation on an ontological level. As Rajiv Kaushik argues, he submits both identity and difference to a diacritically inspired model of meaning that is genuinely multidimensional.[9] This is a point on which the artistic practice of Cy Twombly, in painting and sculpture (which Merleau-Ponty himself did not engage with) can enter into a unique and fruitful interchange with his thought.

As Kirk Varnedoe puts it, Twombly's art foregrounds diverse and sometimes contradictory characteristics, such as "offhand impulsiveness and obsessive systems, the defiling urge toward what is base and the complementary love for lyric poetry and the grand legacy of high Western culture; written words, counting systems, geometry, ideographic signs, and abstract fingerwork with paint."[10] For Roland Barthes, the most subversive of these aspects, is the "jolt" of writing's intrusion into the serene spaciousness of the supposedly pristine pictorial field.[11] The writing that Twombly inscribes there is taken most often from the epic, lyric, and pastoral poetry of ancient Greece and Rome and from the narratives of Mediterranean history, together with the contemporary Greek poetry of Seferis and Cavafy and complemented by the English-language poetry of Spenser, Keats, and T. S. Eliot, and beyond these, in translation, most prominently by Rilke (to say nothing of Twombly's engagement with Japanese haiku, and with Octavio Paz). Perhaps the only intersection of his literary frame of reference with Merleau-Ponty's own concerns the poetics of Stéphane Mallarmé.

To speak of his "taking" texts from these literary traditions is, however, to put the matter far too straightforwardly. Twombly does not simply quote, either casually from memory nor yet accurately from the extensive sources at his disposal, but rather, as Mary Jacobus shows, he works with his favored texts by actively reconfiguring (and thereby defamiliarizing) them.[12] He does so by means of careful (and sometimes even systematic) elisions, or by a substitution of words, or else, conjoining graphics with poetics, by dismembering words to isolate letters, and finally by concentrating the complexities and cultural memory evoked by myth or epic into singular ancient names, such as Orpheus, Dionysus, Achilles, or Virgil.

Given the present focus on the reciprocities between Twombly's oeuvre and Merleau-Ponty's thought, the issues that call for exploration are, most broadly speaking, the interrelations between image and text, and between materiality and ideality. More specifically, they concern the relationships between inscription, quasi-writing, erasure, and coming to presence in the ensuing complexity of marks. Further issues address the self-inscription of the artist's body in mark-making, and the question whether Twombly's preoccupation with the Mediterranean past allows his work to remain relevant to contemporary global concerns. Finally and inescapably, there are the universal issues of mortality, transience, mutability, fragmentation, and the trace that Twombly's art addresses and often foregrounds.

Quasi-Writing, Inscription, Erasure

In advance of Twombly, it was Paul Klee who practiced a "pictorial writing" that, as Kaushik argues, explored the intersection between figure and sign, or between linguistic structure and image, and whose thought and pictorial practice was significant for Merleau-Ponty.[13] In the wider spectrum of mid-twentieth-century abstract art, Mark Tobey drew on Chinese ideographic calligraphy, as well as on Persian and Arabic scripts, for the development of his pictorial "white writing," which was an abstract painterly idiom without legibility. Somewhat similarly, the Chinese-French painter Zao Wou-Ki drew on the forms of archaic Chinese script and on the brushwork of Chinese calligraphic styles in his abstract oil paintings. Merleau-Ponty seems not to have been familiar with either of these artists. Yves Michaud observes aptly, however that, in the 1950s and 1960s, many European and American painters became interested in the nonsignificative use of calligraphic signs because it emancipated them from representation and opened up a new freedom of gesture.[14]

While signification remains integral to both Klee's and Twombly's pictorial writing, it is Twombly whose works require from the viewer a high degree of cultural literacy, and who consistently experiments, according to Jacobus, "within an aesthetic that simultaneously links and disjoins mark-making and meaning-making, sign and reference."[15] The disjunction of calligraphic marks from meaning is emphasized in the rhythms devoid of legibility of Twombly's dark ground or "blackboard" paintings of 1966–1971. Their looping linear choreography explores the ductus and gestural flow of cursive handwriting through a practice of quasi-writing. As Varnedoe notes, they not only present writing's "abstracted, wordless essence," but they also insist on "a driving linear continuity" that Twombly's earlier, as well as continued, practices of mark-making, replete with erotically charged symbols, had excluded.[16] Given the large scale of these works, however, the ductus is not merely that of the writing hand but also of the artist's arm and, indeed, his entire body, giving full expression to Merleau-Ponty's point that, echoing Valéry, "the painter brings his body to the task" (*le peintre apporte son corps*).[17]

Notwithstanding their linear articulation, the "gray ground" paintings are also hauntingly atmospheric. This is due in part to effects of veiling through near-effacement or superposition, together with the subtle nuances of the ground and the varying density or dispersal of linear marks. These veilings call attention to what Merleau-Ponty speaks of as the invisible of the visible, which, notwithstanding the "exactitude" of its articulation (the term was a favorite of Joan Mitchell's, for whom it meant fidelity to feeling[18]) cannot be brought to show itself directly in full presence. By the elusiveness of its presencing, it keeps the sensible, whose "lining and depth" it constitutes, from being misconstrued as sheer "positivity" and thereby impoverished. The carnal idealities that the painter evokes are thus revealed in their horizontal density and scope. The horizon, Merleau-Ponty writes, "is a new type of being, a being of porosity, pregnancy, or of generality"; and he or she for whom the horizon opens is caught up and encompassed within it.[19]

Legibility and its frustration are central to the group of five paintings, each titled individually as *Nini's Painting*, that Twombly created in 1971. These works (in house paint, wax crayon, and pencil on canvas) constitute a threnody for the sudden death by suicide of Nini Pirandello, wife of Twombly's first Roman dealer, Plinio de Martiis. In the obsessive yet lyrical all-over linear entanglements of cursive script or rather quasi-script on subtly hued yet luminous grounds, one can discern fragments of Twombly's own name, and perhaps also of Pirandello's. As Nicholas Cullinan writes, the paintings "seem to embody an absence impossible to articulate." Although they appear to be ever on the verge of speaking to the viewer, they mutely "crumble and dissolve before our gaze."[21] Cullinan also situates the works within the contexts of Twombly's engagement with Robert Burton's *Anatomy of Melancholy* of 1621, and of Leonardo da Vinci's obsessive drawings of tempests and deluges.[21] One may find a further relationship, unintended by Twombly, to Merleau-Ponty's haunting reflection on natality and mortality:

> A human body is there when, between the seer and the visible . . . there comes about a sort of crossing back, when the spark of the sensing-sensible is lit, when the fire takes hold which will not cease to burn until some accident of the body undoes what no accident would have sufficed to create.[22]

Reflecting on Twombly's personal practice, during his military service as a cryptographer in 1953–1954, of drawing in total darkness, as well as with his nondominant hand, Roland Barthes notes that Twombly liberates the graphic trait from ocular control. Thus, according to Barthes, Twombly dissociates painting from vision, given that the "awkwardness (*le 'gauche*') or the wronghandedness (*le 'gaucher'*) of his trait undoes the bond between hand and eye. The consequent warping of his graphic trait yielded "a very mysterious dysgraphy" that remained characteristic of his art.[23]

Since, for Merleau-Ponty, vision and the reciprocities between seer and seen that stem from the seer's self-immersion within the visible are intimately linked not only with the painter's hand but also and especially her mind (allowing here for the resistance of the French *l'esprit* to univocal English translation), one wonders whether Twombly's dysgraphy, as thematized by Barthes, presents a basic challenge to Merleau-Ponty's thought. Far from being fateful, however, the challenge serves to highlight that, for Merleau-Ponty, what a dissociation between eye, mind, and hand puts out of operation is no more than profane vision. To suspend it frees up a rich, primordial, and genuine vision that, as he writes, "is not a certain modality of thought or self-presence: it is the means given to me to be absent from myself, to assist the fission of Being from within . . ."[24]

The fact that profane vision, being habitual, is comforting and reassuring accounts for the difficulty of disabling it by strategies such as sightless drawing. Such practices aim more deeply than the psychic unconscious (in focus for the surrealists) to reach the very event of manifestation, and thus a level at which painting, literature, and the performing arts are not essentially divided. They are rather interconnected by an even wider "*logos of equivalences*" than the one that Merleau-Ponty points to within the visual arts, a *logos* that is revelatory of the event of manifestation and is thus ontological in its import.

The artist Tacita Dean recalls being shown a letter of reference that Twombly had written (by hand, as always). Although the writing was recognizably his own—angular, elegant, yet somewhat dysgraphic—it differed markedly from his inscriptions of text in his paintings since, due to "the intensity of the tremor of communication evident . . . in the context of his art [where] . . . he is *drawing* his words, no longer writing them."[25] One might also say that, in its painterly inscription, the poetic text is being performed, blurring the ordinary distinctions not only between poetry and performance (whose initial union preceded and outlasted the rise of the written epic text[26]), but also between both of these and the image. The confluence of text, performance, and visual image is a new confluence of powers.

Twombly's inscriptions are complemented by a persistent practice of effacement, erasure, encrypting, or defacement (facilitated by the fact that he disliked the viscosity of oil paint and privileged readily erasable pencils, and later acrylic paint). In consequence, works may become palimpsests (like his mid-twentieth-century works *Academy* or *The Geeks*), or else become strictly undecipherable, as in his 1967 group of works on paper titled *Letter of Resignation* (which also raise the issue of the status of signature). Dean observes that manual effacement, however efficient, does not, in contrast to the absolute deletion that can now be effected by technology, utterly cancel the writ but instead gives it the status of a trace. The trace then functions, for the visual artist, as a structural element in the work's creation.[27] The practice of a cancellation that foregrounds the trace is of course akin to the Derridean priority of the *archē*-trace, which usurps and subverts the position of a first and governing principle (*archē*) embodying the ideal of full presence.[28] Focusing specifically on mid-twentieth-century American art, Cullinan observes that, for both Twombly and Rauschenberg, erasure and defacing enabled a break with "the stylish and painterly tropes of Abstract Expressionism" and specifically with the machismo of action painting.[29]

From a Merleau-Pontyan perspective, one finds that effacement, silencing, or obliteration—even where historically or culturally they have barely left a trace—continue to exercise a power of institution.[30] The effaced and obliterated becomes a depth dimension of the invisible of the visible, in the sense in which Merleau-Ponty speaks of it in a 1959 Working Note to *The Visible and the Invisible*:

> The visible itself has a framework [*membrure*] of the invisible, and the invisible is the secret counterpart of the visible; it appears only within it; it is the *Nichturpräsentierbar* which is presented to me as such within the world . . . —one cannot see it there . . . but it is within the sightline of the visible.[31]

The effaced or silenced becomes an aura or a resonance that haunts visual presencing, and of which the visible cannot ultimately divest itself.

Myrtle, Rose, Sparrow . . . /
Laurel, Snake, Grasshopper . . .

These are some of the names of plants and animals associated, respectively, with Aphrodite or Venus and with Apollo that Twombly inscribes on the paired paintings *Venus* and *Apollo* of 1975.[32] Written respectively in sienna and in blue and black on a pale ground, the names of the divinities are roughly traced in labored and superimposed strokes, and the penciled lists of their attributive names and associated plants and animals are likewise roughly executed as though excavated from layers of buried shards and fragments.

In "The Origin of the Work of Art," Heidegger reflects that a Greek temple, firmly grounded upon a rocky promontory, reveals not only the rock's entirely unconstrained supportiveness over against the power and turbulence of the sea but also—and far from exclusively—"the tree and the grass, the eagle and the ox, the snake and the cricket," allowing them in their individuality to come to presence and show themselves as what they are.[33] They show themselves in the context of the historical lifeworld of a people, which cannot, however, be recaptured in identity, given that, as Heidegger acknowledges, the world of the work has already disintegrated *ab initio*. World, he reflects, "is the ever non-objective to which we are submitted, so long as the courses of birth and death, blessing and curse, keep us transported into being [*das Sein*]."[34] The artwork, however, does not simply clarify the parameters of a historical lifeworld but more fundamentally it instigates a strife between "earth" (here a term for the being of beings) and "world," so that the work both "sets up" (*aufstellt*) a world and "sets it back"(*zurückstellt*) into earth (thereby refusing to absolutize it).

Since the artwork, for Heidegger, "belongs as such solely into the domain opened up by itself"[35] (so that the ineluctable disintegration of its original world is not inimical to its revelatory character), and since for him this opening up discloses the past not retrospectively but projectively on the horizon of the future, he has no need for a quasi-archeological labor involving the vagaries of memory and replete with hesitations, defacements, and cancellations, in his efforts to bring to life and give voice again to the art and thought of antiquity. For Twombly, in contrast, the artwork may restrict itself to a bare inscription of names, or even of a single name, such as that of Orpheus or of Virgil. These names, or those of ancient Greek or Egyptian deities, of mythological figures, or those of poets who were the contemporaries of the Presocratic philosophers whom Heidegger privileges, but whom, excepting Homer, he largely ignores—Archilochus, Sappho, or Alkman, rather than Thales, Heraclitus, and Parmenides—are inscribed under a sign of loss. Notwithstanding the extraordinary power of the sheer invocation of names, these inscribed names do not grant access to a world but seem rather to call forth shades out of Hades by the transiently vivifying offering of a gift of paint (rather than the Homeric gift of blood). Even their sonority is muted in favor of their disjoined cadences marked across the work's format. As markers of both a haunting and an insurmountable loss, they certainly do not articulate a Heideggerian intimation of a people's destinal mandate.[36]

Leaving aside here the complex issues of the political import of Heidegger's quest to give voice to the "essential unsaid" of Greek poetic and Presocratic thought, and of the role that, in this context, he assigns to Hölderlin, it is striking that his retrievals nowhere acknowledge the body, either the body of desire and passion or of basic life processes, nor yet the body in pain or the complex life of the body that Plato, never oblivious of it, wants to subject to the educative rigors of *gymnastikē*, and finally the body whose perceptual life and passive subjection to various life processes Aristotle explores. The body, however, foregrounds itself ineluctably in Twombly's art.

The erotic body most obviously, and often transgressively, asserts itself. Cullinan dates "the beginning of the transgressive Twombly" to the start of the 1960s (when Twombly, following his marriage to Luisa Tatiana Franchetti, had taken up residence in Rome).[37] In canvases such as *The Italians* (1961), he deployed a plethora of obsessively reiterated sexual symbols or graphemes—heart shapes doubling as buttocks (with some, as Jacobus puts it, "punctuated by anuses"[38]), breasts, penises, vaginas, and so on—that threaten to fragment the body, possibly beyond any hope of restoring its wholeness or integrity.[39] The fragmentation, however, also attests to the polymorphous character of sexuality. Jacobus, in a detailed commentary on Twombly's painterly engagement with Raphael's frescoes at the Villa Farnesina in Rome and in the Vatican's Stanza della Segnatura, notes that he shows forth what remains not overtly visible in Raphael's "scene of instruction" (in *School of Athens*), namely, "the homoerotic context of Greek pedagogy (and papal courts)."[40] Both Twombly's erotic charge and his almost equally insistent scatology reach a climax in his five *Ferragosto* paintings of 1961, created, as the title implies, during the sweltering month of August in Rome, with its intensification of decay. These paintings are replete not only with an array of sexual symbols but also with stains, globs, smears, and increasingly heavy impasto, in hues of red, flesh pink, and what Cullinan calls "turd brown" (brown, however, connotes for Twombly both the pinnacle of painterly achievement in certain classical masters and the nadir of scatological abjection).[41]

It is important to keep open the span of complexity and ambiguity in the phenomena evoked, and to avoid treating them reductively. As Merleau-Ponty reflects in *Phenomenology of Perception*, sexuality stands in reciprocities of expression with the entire range of sentience, action, and thought.[42] Being thus utterly pervasive in human life, it is irreducible, given that "it is already other than itself; it already is, so to speak, our entire being."[43]

Kaushik argues, furthermore, that the insight (based on Barthes's studies) that Twombly's painterly work shows the gesture, and thereby the body that inscribed the marks, does not entitle one to treat these marks straightforwardly as metaphors "for a set of concrete bodily acts."[44] Instead, he highlights "the continuity between the activity of mark-making and the material on which and in which the marks are inscribed," finding that this continuity makes for a diacritics that resists representational interpretation.[45] One can add further that not only does the artist's body, in inscribing itself, offer no license to reductive literalization, but that it also shows itself everywhere in its indissociable relation to other bodies, including, beyond the human, those of animals and plants. In Greek mythology, this interrelation allowed for a fluidity of metamorphoses, particularly in the context of erotic pursuit and of its avoidance or jealous curtailment.

Addressing War

In 1975, Twombly created two paintings, respectively titled *Apollo and the Artist* and *Mars and the Artist*.⁴⁶ In both, the artist is symbolized by an Egyptian lotus flower sketched onto a rectangular collaged component ("artist" is inscribed close to the flower).⁴⁷ Apollo's name, traced in a palimpsest of blue letters, is placed high above the flower and within another rectangle, slightly decentered. The work is further inscribed with geometrical symbols and numerical measurements, as well as with words such as "poetry" and "music."

In *Mars and the Artist*, strong geometric markings prevail, along with further numerical symbols and suggestions of writing, but the god's name is not placed directly above the artist's lotus. It is situated far to the right and lower down, seemingly pushed there by the force of diagonal markings and by forms suggestive of a convoy of aerial weaponry, such as bombers or missiles. The god's name is split into the large and assertive initial M (which is further divided by a line extending from the rectangle's right margin) and the smaller *ars*, which (notwithstanding its connotation of "arse" that tends to dominate critical commentary) is Latin for "art." Twombly thus acknowledges that, in some ways, but not by Apollonian inspiration, the violence of war is and long has been a source of art and that, at least in the pairing of these collages, the juxtaposition of Apollo and Mars calls into question the Nietzschean juxtaposition of the Apollinian and Dionysian art energies.

Twombly scholarship is profoundly indebted to Jacobus's insightful argumentation to the effect that the prevailing view of Twombly's art as essentially lyrical and preoccupied with Mediterranean history, mythology, and culture (including, of course, the mythical and historic wars deeply embedded in Mediterranean memory and imagination) is inadequate. As she writes, "Twombly—whose work has often been read as transcendently poetic and mythic, and hence as both ahistorical and apolitical—uses the past dialectically to interrogate aspects of modernity; the image is not so much archaic as disruptive."⁴⁸

One Twombly scholar, however, Joshua Rivkin, remains skeptical about Twombly's works ever really addressing war or issues such as the ravages of the AIDS epidemic, noting that Twombly's "natural inclination" was not oriented toward sociopolitical issues.⁴⁹ Nonetheless, the Vietnam and Iraq wars, in particular, as well as AIDS (which took a heavy toll on American artistic and intellectual life) would have been almost impossible to ignore or sideline by an artist of Twombly's fine-tuned sensibility and personal intensity (although they, and other contemporary issues and traumas, may well have been transposed onto the Mediterranean past or encrypted).

Although Merleau-Ponty, in the opening section of "Eye and Mind," portrays the painter as being absolved from "the responsibilities of speaking man" and thus at license to practice painting as a proto-phenomenological "secret science" endeavoring to reach "the fabric of brute meaning" that subtends human constructs,[50] such an understanding of painting's privilege is neither in harmony with the philosopher's own recognition that the political dimension is all-pervasive within human experience and thus within phenomenology, nor yet, to a significant extent, with painterly practice.

Even though not all of Twombly's works concerned with the narratives of Mediterranean wars can be straightforwardly seen as indirect engagements with contemporary events—thus for instance his *Lepanto* series of 2001 is, by his own characterization, concerned primarily with color (and thus with painterly issues) as well as with his iconic boat motif[51]—such an engagement is crucial to at least three of his important series or groups of works: *Fifty Days at Iliam* of 1977–1978, certain sculptures of 1991–1992, and the Bacchus cycles of paintings of 2004–2005.

Twombly had already engaged with Homer's *Iliad* in single works of 1962 and 1964, among them *Vengeance of Achilles* (Kunsthaus Zürich) and *Ilium, One Morning Ten Years Later* (private collection). The first of these condenses the figure of Achilles into the avowedly phallic form of the initial A of his name, which is also, in Jacobus's words, "an abstract, fire-tipped weapon somewhere between a gigantic javelin and a rocket trailing tendrils of smoke."[52] The second work, which is contemporaneous with the escalation of the Vietnam War and the Gulf of Tonkin Resolution, shows the Trojan battlefield as no more than a scene of detritus and of a confused tangle of sexual and scatological signifiers.

Fifty Days at Iliam (Philadelphia Museum of Art), a major cycle of paintings in ten parts whose creation, as Twombly tells Serota, he had "a terrible time with,"[53] was inspired by Alexander Pope's verse translation of the *Iliad*. As Varnedoe points out, it constitutes Twombly's first effort to create a historical ensemble since the extremely hostile critical reception of his earlier group of paintings, *Discourses on Commodus*, shown in New York in 1964.[54] To cite Jacobus once more, however, "the work is also date-stamped with its own historical moment: the immediate aftermath of the Vietnam War."[55]

The vengeance of Achilles for the death of Patroclus (which he knew would cost him his own life) remains central to Twombly's painterly meditation on war (with his deliberate misspelling of Ilium as "Iliam" further stressing the phallic aggression of the A of the hero's name). In part 5 of the series, at its most powerful, this aggression becomes "The Fire That Consumes All Before It," shown as a brilliant red, black-centered flame that juts horizontally into the vertical panel from the right. However, this aggression is contested, in part 9, by "Shades of Eternal Night," so that, according to Jacobus, "phallus and cloud/shade compete for dominance . . . along with a circular scribble . . . that characterizes Homer's embattled warriors and the shield of Achilles."[56] The cloud/shade sign stands not only for the dead—specifically, in part 7, for Achilles, Patroclus, and Hector—but also for the call for commemoration or memorialization, without which there remains, perhaps, next to nothing, or just the distressing detritus of *One Morning, Ten Years After*, of historically decisive battles and of individual heroism and agony (which is today largely effaced by mechanized aerial warfare).

There remains, nonetheless, the mythological shield of Achilles, fashioned by Hephaestus, which depicts the still horizonal order of the polis in which the lawful adjudication of disputes can supervene upon vengeance or retribution. It may be that Homer's inability to envisage this order—an inability largely shared by the tragedians whom he inspired—is a reason for Plato's censure of the Homeric epics and of tragedy, and thus of their banishment from the ideal city.[57]

Discussing the hermeneutic fecundity of works of art, Merleau-Ponty stresses that the work itself opens up the horizons over against which it can appear in another light, so that the continuing reinterpretations to which it is prone "change it only into itself."[58] One can glimpse this hermeneutic fecundity at work with respect to Twombly's sculptures of 1991–1992, whose critical engagement with war has only recently, and not univocally, come to be recognized.[59] One such sculpture, *Thicket*, of 1991 (there are four versions of *Thicket*), consists of a fragile treelike form, painted white, with gardeners' wooden tags for leaves and with a trunklike, narrowly vertical rectangle that is inscribed with the names of ancient and lost or ruined Sumerian cities. Whereas Cullinan interprets it in terms of Twombly's interest in and knowledge of Sumerian antiquity, conjoined with his pastoral streak,[60] both Lewison and Jacobus see it in a different light. The sculpture is one of a group contemporaneous with the First Gulf War, and Twombly not only memorializes the destroyed ancient sites within a region recognized as the cradle of Western civilization but also addresses, in Jacobus's words, "the hideous spectacle of the Highway of Death."[61]

Epitaph, consisting of a rough wooden box coated and filled to overflowing with white plaster, is inscribed with the grim and sardonic verses of Archilochus about the hospitality of war that leaves behind corpses as a gift for remembrance. This "gift," as Jacobus observes, "travesties both gift and memorial."[62] Finally, *Thermopylae*, inscribed with Cavafy's verses, memorializes not only the Spartan army's defeat, due to betrayal, in the pass of Thermopylae in 480 BCE, but also the betrayal inherent in the loss of soldiers' lives in war.[63] The sculpture is a tumulus—vaguely reminiscent in form of an ancient Greek helmet—from which rise four unopened tuliplike blooms that, according to Lewison, are emblematic of young lives cut down before they could reach their potential.[64]

In 2004–2005, Twombly created two cycles of paintings focused on the Dionysian theme of *Bacchus, Psilax, Mainomenos* (*Bacchus, Winged, Raving Mad*).[65] These paintings, in vermillion on a pale ochre ground, are sheer manifestations of energy asserting itself in soaring loops or frenzied coils. They are painted in acrylic used in a fluid state, so that gravity asserts itself (counteracting the energies of both flight and rampant madness) in pervasive drips that, in some cases (where the wet canvas was folded close to the bottom so as to be moved), coagulate into horizontal striated marks. Jacobus notes that these paintings were done during the bloodiest years of the Iraq War (an emblematic war of vengeance in which, in contrast to Achilles's vengeful and brutal abuse of Hector's corpse, the vengeance was displaced). Nonetheless, while it is important to recognize, with Jacobus, that "Twombly's martial art underlines the human destruction entwined with the heroic *mythos* of Homer's *Iliad*,"[66] to read these cycles solely in relation to war would be reductive, and thus limiting. Although Merleau-Ponty, whose death preceded Twombly's by fifty years, could not, leaving aside cultural and geographic differences, have addressed his mature art, his thought nonetheless opens up a wider perspective by asking how static, three-dimensional images or sculptures can communicate the energy of motion.

In "Eye and Mind," Merleau-Ponty answers this question chiefly in terms of Rodin's insight that showing a body in motion involves showing the parts of its anatomy in positions that are incompossible in simultaneity, thus making manifest motion's dynamic temporality:

> The painting makes one see motion by its internal discordance; the position of each member, precisely by what makes it incompatible with those of others according to the logic of

the body—is dated otherwise; and since they all remain visible within the unity of the body, it is the body that begins to bestride duration.[67]

Twombly is not, of course, concerned to show bodies in motion, but motion is not merely evoked but also emphatically enacted by the rhythms of gesture, by lines that do not outline but that dramatically effract trajectories, or by pictorial elements that rush, glide, or drift through the picture space and may be truncated by its edges.

Drawing largely on Merleau-Ponty's 1947 essay, "The Film and the New Psychology,"[67] Mauro Carbone adopts the philosopher's own terminology in characterizing a filmic work as "a temporal *Gestalt*."[69] Its unitary import exceeds the complex totality of its component parts and, in emerging from its spatiotemporal structure, it reveals consciousness to be "thrown into the world" and to be indissociable from the body and from others.[70] Hence, as Carbone stresses, motion inscribes itself "both on the exterior and the interior side of experience."[71] In his second lecture course on Nature, focused on animality, Merleau-Ponty similarly explores organismic unity with reference to the excess of wholes over the totality of their parts, characterizing this issue as fundamental not only to biology but to philosophy itself.[72] The issue of the whole/part relation is one that Merleau-Ponty scholarship still needs to address, given its centrality to his thought.

In Twombly's Dionysian cycles of paintings, and ultimately in the final and related cycle, *Camino Real*, that he worked on up to his death, he gives one to see and viscerally to experience the dynamism of sheer, primordial energy—its fiery nature checked by the gravity-bound fluidity of paint—while also touching, through the unity of a temporal *Gestalt*, on some of the philosophical and specifically phenomenological issues highlighted by Merleau-Ponty.

The Elements

The history of philosophy, Merleau-Ponty observes, offers no name by which meaningfully to designate the ontological notion of flesh that his late thought strives to articulate. Flesh is neither matter nor spirit, nor yet substance or mental representation. Instead of these standard exclusionary philosophical concepts, he resorts to the ancient notion of element, calling flesh "an element of Being" in the sense in which it was used to speak of water, of air, of earth, and of fire, which is to say in the sense of a *general* thing, midway between the spatio-temporal individual and the idea, a sort of incarnate principle that brings with it a style of being wherever one finds a particle of it.⁷³

Within the elementality of flesh, Merleau-Ponty indicates reversibilities, the terms of which are clearly (and significantly) not straightforwardly interchangeable. One cannot, according to Renaud Barbaras, let the world appear without being already situated within its depths, in an inherence that he terms "hyper-belonging" (*hyper-appartenance*).⁷⁴ The "hyper," as an asymmetrical mark of excess, frustrates inherence or belonging by the recognition of a persistent gap, deviation, or *écart* as a mark of nonclosure.⁷⁵

Since Merleau-Ponty's concern is to explore the elementality of flesh ontologically, he does not discuss the elements as recognized by Presocratic thought in their distinctive character—the *rhizomata*, for instance, to which Empedocles gave mythical and sacred names, or the Heraclitean fire and elemental cycles of transformation. He therefore does not address the ways in which painting, throughout its history, has given expression to the human experience of elemental energies; but these are, in contrast, at the forefront of Twombly's art. Of the four elements considered by ancient thought to embody the fundamental "styles of being"—earth, water, fire, and air—his art privileges fire and water, notwithstanding their antithetical character (this privileging may constitute the deeper reason for the frequent association of his paintings, in historical perspective, with those of Turner and Monet). Space—recognized as elemental in certain Asian traditions of thought—is scarcely less fundamental for Twombly. Tacita Dean recognizes its importance without explicitly naming it. She speaks instead of Twombly's adherence to "the principle of *white*; whether white be that of paint or bare canvas, his white is in a standoff with the clumps, the smudges, and the scribbles . . ."⁷⁶ She further notes that the sparseness or spaciousness of Twombly's art is connected to a silence "that is both welcome and unbearable, not unlike oblivion."⁷⁷ Like space itself, it is welcome or welcoming because it enables all presencing, but it also dissolves and obliterates it, leaving only the possibility of its evocation, along with the trace.

The element most conspicuously in focus for Twombly is water—from *Poems to the Sea* of 1959 to the *Hero and Leandro* sequence of 1981–1984, together with *Hero and Leandro (to Christopher Marlowe)* of 1985, and on to the *Green Paintings* with their Rilkean "ponds broken off from the sky."⁷⁸

Expanses of water—whether the oceans, lakes, or rivers of the planet's geography or the mythical watercourses of the ancient Greek underworld—are the domain of boats whose iconic forms and symbolism of leave-taking, passage, Odyssean errancy, homecoming, and ultimate departure are abidingly fascinating and oneirically compelling for Twombly. His boat images, however, frequently conjoin, as already suggested, an evocation of the aqueous element with the antithetical element of fire, as in the burning boats of the Lepanto series, or in works such as *Leaving Paphos Ringed with Waves* (titled after a verse by Alkman), with its fiery boat shapes moving through "waves" of turquoise interspersed with yellow script.[79] In this context, one also needs to include his 1981 *Gaeta Set (for the Love of Fire and Water)* that was conjoined with *Eight Poems* by Octavio Paz to form an artist's book.[80]

Elemental earth is manifest in Twombly's art from the outset as ancient or eroded surfaces and strata (so that the format of the palimpsest shows itself to be connected with earth). Given the dense materiality of the "heavy" body (*le corps lourd*, as Merleau-Ponty sometimes calls it), it is also allied to the markings and smears applied directly by the artist's hands. Importantly, it is further expressed by the vegetal domain to which Twombly was always attentive.[81] This expression conjoins the elemental energies into an astonishing achievement of efflorescence. Twombly's late, almost monumental images of peonies or roses, inscribed (sometimes on the borderline of legibility) with fragments of the poetry of T. S. Eliot, Rilke, Emily Dickinson, Ingeborg Bachmann, or even with haiku,[82] interlink the liquidity of broadly brushed loops and squiggles with both vegetal earthiness and the solar fire that reveals the spectrum's chromas. In the words of Eliot's "Little Gidding," recalled by Cullinan, the paintings evoke an enfolding of "the tongues of flame," in a vision in which "the fire and the rose are one."[83]

The elements as traditionally understood constitute the fundamental styles of sensible presencing and are thus basic to experience. As Kaushik argues, the being of beings, even when understood as flesh, lacks self-containment or self-sufficiency and thus cannot be set apart from beings by an ontological difference. Rather, it must constantly be figured forth into beings in their multiply different modalities of presencing.[84] Even the elemental styles of presencing lack self-sufficiency, and Presocratic thought concerning the elements indicates this by its emphasis on elemental transmutation and cosmic cycles. Heraclitus's fragment B 31, for instance, shows these transformations to be unimpeded by the antithetical character of the elements. It reads (in translation that cannot do justice to Heraclitus's verbal artistry): "Turning-points of fire: first sea; of sea, the half earth, and the half burning wind [*prēstēr*]; sea extends itself throughout and is measured according to the same *logos* that obtained at first."[85]

An explication that could hope to do justice to the fragment calls for scholarship that is beyond the scope of this chapter. If however one thinks of the elements in transformation as energies manifesting themselves through light giving rise to the spectrum, one gains a new perspective on Octavio Paz's comment that Twombly "wants to see *through* the image," and that therefore his paintings "have to do with light."[86] To see, not just the image, but *through* the image (which, in this sense, is a seeing opposed to the ideal of sheer transparency) is to see aspects of what Merleau-Ponty speaks of as the invisible of the visible, and thus to encounter, in sensible presencing, the differential light energies of manifestation.

Chapter 4

Resonances of Silence and the Dimension of Color

The Art of Joan Mitchell

> By the disintegration of the figurative, one finds a Beauty which is sought by painting's internal exigency, and which no longer hides pain and death, being the profound sensitivity [*fibre*] thereto.
>
> —Maurice Merleau-Ponty, *Notes de cours*

Joan Mitchell held that paintings cannot be "read" or rearticulated equivalently in language. Certainly if, in accordance with Paul Klee's *Creative Credo*, painting *renders visible* aspects of experience that, being properly concerned with the invisible of the visible, would otherwise remain incapable of communication,[1] its focus cannot then be trained on representation (which does not resist language). Mitchell's insistence on painting's elision of language, together with her frequent retreat into inarticulateness when called upon to discuss her work, is particularly intriguing, given that she was a devoted and sophisticated reader of literature, and especially of lyric poetry. Her art responded, in particular, to the poetry of Wordsworth, Rilke, T. S. Eliot, Wallace Stevens, Jacques Dupin, Frank O'Hara, and James Schuyler, to say nothing of her close and sustained friendship with Samuel Beckett. Resorting to the words of Claude Lefort, commenting on Merleau-Ponty's reading of the novelist Claude Simon (and thus of comments that cross and recross the dividing line between verbal and silent art), her quest might be understood as akin to Simon's seeking "the passage . . . to a non-figurative writing" that strives to reveal "the *magma* of which [things] as well as we are part."² In this sense, language, as what Mauro Carbone speaks of as "a showing by words," comes rather to be "the resonance of the silence in which the sensible dwells."³ Reading Claude Simon, one might also say that it is the sheer fulguration of the sensible, commingled with changing intensities or relaxations of feeling, that ultimately constitutes one's experience of reality, time, and history, so that all of these constituents (and the experience of space should certainly be included) remain as imperceptible, in their intrinsic being and effects, as, to stay with Simon's own comparison) the growth of grass.⁴

Although Mitchell drew inspiration from poetry, she insisted on the autonomy of painterly creation. As she stressed in her interviews with Yves Michaud,⁵ and as Merleau-Ponty also recognizes in his meditations on line or on color in "Eye and Mind," painting consists first of all of formal elements that are proper to it or to visual art, such as color or forms in space, articulated within the materiality of its medium (or media). Much of the excitement of the painting process, as well as its challenges, arise from the dynamic interaction between these components.

Nonetheless, as Merleau-Ponty affirmed, painting must maintain a relationship with the world—a relationship that enables it "not to copy, [but rather] to give the essence."⁶ In the absence of such a relationship, painting could not claim genuine autonomy but would rather "fall back on itself," much like a thing traditionally understood, into inertness and irrelevance.⁷ Unlike Heidegger in "The Origin of the Work of Art," Merleau-Ponty does not thematize an enigmatic kinship between the "mere things" of nature and works of art that instigate a "strife" between "world," conceived as the lifeworld of a historical people, and "earth" as a granting or withholding of manifestation or presencing that, as such, remains inexplicable. For Merleau-Ponty, the genuine artwork has no kinship either to mere things or to a historical lifeworld, but rather, in its engagements with these, it transcends them and achieves a universality that remains without concept. Mitchell's art, being resolutely nonfigurative, draws on an engagement with the world that is rooted primarily in her deeply felt experience of and response to landscape and to the phenomena of nature (which, however, she did not dissociate from the built environment prior to her move to France in 1959).⁸

When Mitchell purchased a property in Vétheuil, France, in 1967 (it became her permanent residence the following year), the responsiveness of her art to nature (and specifically to landscape and light, which she now shared with Monet) encouraged facile comparisons of her art to the impressionist master's, whose modest residence from 1878 to 1881 formed part of her property. She was, perhaps excessively, at pains to reject this association (even though she readily acknowledged her debt to other painters, including van Gogh, Cézanne, and Matisse). Like Monet, she had an abiding fascination with the element of water, but unlike him, she did not seek to capture the ever-changing appearances of water nor of nature generally (which for Monet also often included built structures) due to light and atmospheric effects.[9] Rather, she distilled the complexities and intensities of memory and feeling in response to nature into images that would be "exact" in being emotionally true to them. Memory here is not a matter of references to an objectively given, self-contained past but foregrounds, rather, the continued efficacy of a past that was shaped, from the outset, by imagination and by the oneiric dimension and that thus was therefore never straightforwardly present.[10] Rather, in the merging of remembered qualities of feeling with her current responses to nature or landscape, Mitchell achieved an institution of place that counteracted her own visceral sense of displacement or of being constantly in need of maps and geographical coordinates to have a sense of her own identity.[11] Apart from this issue of a search for emplacement, Klaus Kertess also points out the fact that Mitchell's emphatic affirmation of emotion and of a carnal participation in the world counteracted Clement Greenberg's contemporaneous critical rejection of content or emotion in favor of pure opticality.[12]

Linda Nochlin notes perceptively that Mitchell's work achieves meaning and emotional resonance through painterly oppositions that, far from being ultimately resolved in a manner that would approach the placid inertness of things (let alone art-market commodities), remain dynamically and precariously in tension.[13] The most prominent opposition highlighted in her work is that between chaotic disintegration and the achievement of an intuitive and tenuous order; but one can also point out bravura versus delicacy, or forceful gestural work in tension with atmospheric veilings. More generally and importantly, Mitchell explored the dynamic tensions in figure/ground ambiguities that characterize much of contemporary nonfigurative painting, but which Merleau-Ponty, committed as he was to the ultimacy of the figure/ground articulation in Gestalt psychology, may not have fully appreciated.[14] Mitchell's working process, for all her virtuoso brushwork suggesting sheer spontaneity, was actually deliberate and reflective. Despite the freedom of her paint handling, as well as her extensive use of drips (she painted on canvases positioned vertically and often thinned her paints with turpentine), she did not, as she put it with characteristic bluntness, "go off and slop and drip."[15] She took up positions at a distance from work in progress (aided by a diminishing glass) and meditated her next move or stroke, often for long periods of time.

Notwithstanding the abstract expressionist heritage of her gestural abstraction (she cultivated close friendships with Franz Kline and Willem de Kooning), Mitchell diverged from this heritage not only by her unconcern with subjectivity, the sublime, or the inspiration of myth, but importantly in her commitment to beauty. She considered her work, or her painterly sensibility, to have an affinity to that of Agnes Martin,[16] for whom beauty was the central "mystery of life," notwithstanding the disparity between Mitchell's gestural freedom, or what Kertess aptly characterizes as the "unsettled ecstasy" of her best work,[17] and Martin's contrasting basic commitment to the mathematics and felt "innocence" of the grid. Whereas Martin (whose religious and intellectual references included Calvinism as well as Zen Buddhism and Taoism) sought a Platonically inspired beauty of transcendent perfection, disencumbered of passions and of sensory clutter, Mitchell's beauty remains resolutely in contact with this world and its passions, ambiguities and imperfections; and it is often menaced and pained. Nonetheless, Mitchell's and Martin's understandings of beauty as realized by visual art converge in their emphasis on an oblivion of self, which Martin speaks of as emptiness and humility, whereas Mitchell (an accomplished athlete in her youth) compares it to riding a bicycle without using one's hands.[18]

Color, Whiteness, and Light

In "Eye and Mind," Merleau-Ponty speaks of "the dimension of color," out of and within which there arise "identities, differences, a texture, a materiality,[19] and ultimately a coming into presences of being itself, without concept. Mitchell reflects that "what excites me as I paint is what one color does to another color and what both of them do in terms of space and interaction." She adds that she responds emotionally to configurations of colors on a plane surface, and that the formal elements of painting are inherently imbued with feeling.[20] If her acknowledgment of the interdependence of visual registers, and indeed of the interdependence of single elements within a given register, such as form, space, color, tonality, or line, is in keeping with Merleau-Ponty's recognition of a "*logos* of equivalences" in visual art, her own emphasis is placed more strongly on the ensuing play of ambivalences and ambiguities than on sheer equivalence. Chief among these there is, as already noted, the ambiguity of figure and ground, as well as that between both maintaining and negating a horizon, which she stresses in her conversation with Michaud.[21]

Whereas some painters work within a recognizably constant chromatic register (such as van Gogh's mature dominant yellows, blues, and cool greens), Mitchell's chromatic "keys" (the musical metaphor is apt given her passion for music) are highly variable over different periods of her work. In just a rough and lacunary outline, they comprise the subtle neutral tones of grays and umbers, and the shimmering pale tonalities that, as Bernstock aptly puts it, "disembody the Cubist structure" of her work of the early 1950s,[22] in contrast to the strong primary colors (red, yellow, and blue) she used later in the decade. Iconic paintings of that period are *George Went Swimming* (1956, Albert Knox Gallery) and the powerful *To the Harbormaster* (The Graham Gund Charitable Trust).[23] The later 1960s brought her somber "black paintings" that, however, contain no pigmentary blacks. In contrast, the paintings that she created after her move to Vétheuil exhibit vibrant chromatic intensity, and often a preponderance of yellow. Examples include *My Landscape, II* (National Museum of American Art) and her *Sunflower* paintings of this period.

Although no single chromatic key characterizes Mitchell's work of the 1970s, which in her *Fields and Territories*, affirms a gridlike structure, blue is often privileged. It may be complemented by orange, juxtaposed to massive near-blacks, or conjoined, particularly in paintings with marine associations such as *Mooring* (1971, collection of Harriet K. Ewing, Providence, Rhode Island) with teals and atmospheric hues. Mitchell's complex and masterful paint handling heightens the chromatic richness of these works. Blue remains in focus in her works of the later 1970s, which relinquish structure for a dense, all-over mode of painting, as in *Aires pour Marion* (1975–1976, collection of Phil Schrager, Omaha, Nebraska) or *A Place for Puppies* (1975–1976, the Solomon R. Guggenheim Museum).[24] Like the *Fields and Territories* paintings, or like *Chasse Interdite* (1973, Robert Miller Gallery), these works extend Mitchell's concern for an establishment of place in a quest for protected places as sanctuaries.

The early years of the 1980s were, for Mitchell, a time of traumatic personal losses, marked by the deaths of her psychoanalyst and close friend Edrita Fried, and of her sister Sally Perry, following closely upon the end of her relationship of over twenty years with the Canadian painter Jean-Paul Riopelle in 1979. As she had done in the mid-1960s, which brought the deaths of her parents and of both Franz Kline and Frank O'Hara, she immersed herself intensely in painting as being, for her, not only a necessity and obsession but also, as she tells Michaud, what enabled her to remain in touch with her own vitality.[25] Important works of the early 1980s often foreground strong yellows, oranges, and deep violet blue, leading on to the chromatic intensities and their emotional resonance in her sequence of works of 1983–1984, *La Grande Vallée* (The big valley). As a compelling and culminating achievement, this sequence demands, and will here shortly receive, a focused discussion.

Mitchell's late works are often characterized by a ferocious turbulence, and even though aesthetic balance is precariously achieved, it remains in extreme tension with the sense one has of witnessing an explosive and shattering event. Mitchell's titles now are often minimalist, elliptical and challenging, such as *Then, Last Time* or *Before, Again*, evoking time and mortality, while her color may tend toward acidic dissonance, as in *Faded Air* (1985, collection of Thomas and Arlene Furst). Blacks may be juxtaposed to icy yellow and conjoined with rust, mauve, and cobalt green in her calligraphy of strokes. Pigmentary black is now prominent, as are both deep and faded blues, a muted orange, and a dark green. Notwithstanding this "subversive toxicity" of chromas, as Kertess calls it,[26] Mitchell's late work does not move toward bleakness. Instead, in her oil paintings—diptychs being now her preferred format—as well as in a body of large-scale pastels, and in her printmaking projects, she achieves a commanding mastery of color and light, as well as of gesture and space, in their full expressive power.

Merleau-Ponty reflects that Cézanne's late practice of leaving areas of canvas, gessoed white but unpainted, interspersed among his colors (he cites here in particular a late portrait of the gardener Vallier) points to the artist's awareness of "a more general being of color" than do the various constellations of chromas.[27] His reflection is puzzling in that, in the context of discussing oil painting and thus pigmentary color, he seems nonetheless to be pointing to the inclusion of the colors of the spectrum within pure white light, and thus to speak of, or at least to allude to, spectral color. Perhaps, somewhat speculatively, one could understand the inclusive generality of white that he speaks of as indicating that the painter's work takes shape within the visible as its "concentration and coming to itself,"[28] and thus in analogy to the spectral colors arising within, and out of, white light, which could thus be characterized as fully coming to itself. If so, this reflection offers another perspective on Merleau-Ponty's view that modern painting moves toward becoming autofigurative.[29]

Mitchell's painting is characterized, on the whole, by a near-constant and extensive use of white, which is most often achieved by pigmentary color Mitchell personally associated white, in particular a certain "metallic" white, with illness, hospitalization, death, loss, and creative sterility.[30] Nonetheless, far from scrupulously avoiding white, she treated the dreaded achromatic color (though perhaps not the "metallic" white that she abhorred) as fundamental to her chromatic and formal articulation, recalling how silence is fundamental to speech. As Bernstock points out (speaking of Mitchell's work of 1956), white is also essential to her creation of figure/ground ambiguity or irresolution: "By varying the amount of white and also the quality of line or stroke interacting with it, Mitchell explores different ways of defying the traditional static relationship between positive and negative."[31] In this context, Mitchell uses the visually advancing or receding qualities of chromas (as well as of their tonalities) in the context of exploring white (which is inherently advancing and expansive) to explore ambiguities concerning positive and negative space, and thus also within the figure/ground relation, leaving them, once again, without resolution.

Weaving in and out of chromas, underlying or subtly mingling with them, contained by them or else surrounding them, overpainted or scumbled, forming vast expanses or reduced to flickers and filigree traceries, Mitchell's whites do not, in and of themselves, give luminosity to her paintings. Luminosity is one of her key concerns but is not tantamount to brightness. If her whites are essential to the luminosity of her work, they are so not in themselves but rather by virtue of their interactions with chromas.

Mitchell explicitly denied that light in painting has anything to do with the use of white. Matisse, in her view, "had light"; but she granted genuine "light" neither to Monet, who used flickers of white in the context of conveying atmospheric luminosity, nor yet, further back in history, to the luminist painter Georges de la Tour (1593–1652) whose paintings often show candle flames dramatically illuminating the darkness.[32] Her whites not only allow chromas to reveal their inherent luminosity, but they also allow complementary colors to generate light by their mediated juxtaposition, without the distracting optical flicker effects that can ensue when they are immediately adjacent.

As Nochlin points out, brightness and radiance in Mitchell's work are generally menaced by "streaks of hovering darkness."[33] Her light is a shadowed light, in contrast to the shadowless brilliance of the Platonic sun, as well as of the Cartesian *lumen naturale* (natural light), both of which are accessible only to the pure intellect divorced from sensuousness as well as from feeling. Carbone thus speaks of "light that can illuminate the flesh . . . only insofar as it is diffused by the flesh itself."[34] Painting has, throughout its history, explored the "structural luminosity" of flesh, even if one needs perhaps to turn to "modern" (twentieth-century?) painting's disencumbering itself of representational and narrative expectations to realize fully "the profound discordance," or the "mutation in the relations of man and Being" that Merleau-Ponty discerns in the confrontation of the researches of modern painting with "the universe of classical thought."[35]

Mortal Flesh

Except for still life photography, Mitchell considered painting to be the only nontemporal art. Painting alone, she tells Michaud, does not come to an end, and motion within a painting is immobilized "like a fish caught in ice." Hence, she explains, she herself spontaneously immobilizes experience as it is happening by "enframing" it, changing it from a mutable segment of life to a self-contained *image*. She recalls visiting a Manet exhibition when she was traumatized by her sister's death of cancer in 1982 and feeling enveloped and embraced by silence there, released from time and limitations. She comments that "it was marvellous."[36] Despite the dynamism of her brushwork, she evidently valued a certain stillness and did not share Merleau-Ponty's concern for painting's ability to convey the actuality or essentiality of motion.

In commenting on the affinity between Mitchell's painting and O'Hara's poetry (an affinity of which both poet and painter were aware), Bernstock's interpretation diverges somewhat from Mitchell's own statements. Bernstock writes that, whereas O'Hara sought aesthetic cohesion within the "formlessness" of experience, Mitchell sought to unite "a oneness of the image with constant motion."[37] Mitchell's sense of the temporality of experience, implicit in motion, was that of transience, finitude, and loss, and thus of the condition of mortality. To unite it with the singularity and stability of the image involved "enframing" and thus stilling this ceaseless transience. She seems to have understood temporality as ceaseless succession, and thus as evanescence; but Merleau-Ponty, no more than Heidegger, is willing to accept a notion of time as sheer passage and a linear succession of singular moments (which is the Cartesian understanding of time, in contrast to yet connected with a continuity of space understood as extension). Merleau-Ponty explores temporality, in a manner mediated by the literary work of Claude Simon, in terms of encroachments, reciprocal precession, and "the cohesion of incompossibles." Time and space, he reflects, "are horizons and not series of things."[38]

Specifically, what he calls "the flesh of the world" is not just a metaphor for one's bodily participation in the bodily life of the world, but rather, human life and the experience of time or space are constituted of the same *magma* (Simon's term).[39] Within this *magma*, "time is encapsulation [*emboîtement*]; the present (always sensible as well as spatial) holds within its depths other presents." There is, furthermore, an inter-encroachment (*empiètement*) of bodies, so that what happens to one of them, "in the promiscuity of birth, of love, and of death," changes the duration of others.[40] The analysis implicitly negates not only the shadowless brilliance of the Platonic sun but also the Platonic ideal of the self-sufficiency of the philosopher or the realized man (*epieikēs anēr*), who is supposedly impervious not only to the afflictions that may personally befall him, but also to the misfortunes and sufferings of others, even if they are his immediate family or close friends.[41]

Even though Mitchell does not verbally articulate an understanding of the temporality of experience in its interinvolved and multidimensional complexities, her art gives expression to it. This is particularly true of her suite of twenty-one paintings, *La Grande Vallée*. The impetus for these works (which are now dispersed) was yet another death within a period in which she suffered major personal losses: the death of a cousin of her close friend, the composer Gisèle Barreau. Barreau had communicated to Mitchell her own treasured memory of a wild, secluded valley in her native Brittany that was her childhood refuge and sanctuary. She had, at the time, shared this refuge with only one other person, her cousin Jean-Philippe who now, at age twenty-eight, had died of cancer. His final wish had been to see again this secret "great valley," but due to his precarious condition, the wish could not be fulfilled.

In the suite *La Grande Vallée*, Mitchell adopts an all-over approach: the canvases (which include five diptychs and one triptych) are filled edge to edge with brushwork, in short and swirling strokes rather than in her more customary expansive arcing ones, and in ecstatically intense color. White has now lost its predominance and much of its structurally organizing function; it is reduced to small patches, flickers, streaks, or marginal areas of bare canvas (in contrast to Mitchell's customary pigmentary whites) that bear the colored drip marks of wet paint. One has the sense that all points of entry to Mitchell's dreaded metallic and sterile white, the emblem of death, have been foreclosed. Despite the agitation of her brushstrokes and the paintings' emotional intensity, they nonetheless each create what Mitchell calls "a quiet place,"[42] communicating an affirmation of life in the full realization of its fragility. They also offer themselves as a tenuous recreation of the childhood experience of an enchanted valley—a recreation that does not lose sight of trauma and of mortality, which is at least as much the trauma of others' deaths than of "my death" (which Heidegger privileges). They may also offer a vision of the "great valley" as a memorial abode for souls or spirits, particularly those of Sally and Jean-Philippe, that lies ultimately "beyond life and death."[43] The vision is not escapist, and even if it opens up a transcendent dimension, it still recalls and cherishes the sensory intensities of this world: the colors and fragrances of wild flowers, the freshness or saturation of spring's or summer's greens, and the sonority of the voices of birds, frogs, and insects, along with the sounds of wind.

The dominant color of the *Grande Vallée* suite is blue—a blue that ranges from Cézanne's milky blues (in some of his images of bathers) to intense cobalt, cerulean, and ultramarine and to a dark blue-violet. These are conjoined with their complementaries or near-complementaries, which are yellow and orange hues, and are also interwoven with greens and sometimes rose or violet-rose. These luminous colors are, however, often opposed and contested by black, which encroaches in massed and seemingly menacing formations. Despite their restrictive effect, however, these blacks do not ultimately prevail. Indeed, in some paintings within the suite, such as *La Grande Vallée V (Jean)* (collection of Jean Fournier), the blacks ascending from below are partly overlaid and, as it were, held in check by, yellows that themselves ascend toward increasingly ethereal blues. In other canvases, strong yellows predominate and almost push the black marks out of the picture. As Kertess points out, the constants in Mitchell's art are her commitment to beauty and her love of the materiality of painting.[44] In the *La Grande Vallée* suite, beauty communicates by its visual intensity and through painterly registers such as form, line, color, and space, to the depth levels of human sensibility.

Carnal Essences

A 1989 exhibition of Mitchell's then current work at New York's Robert Miller Gallery comprised some canvases small enough to be visually encompassed by, rather than encompassing, the viewer.[45] Mitchell's titles at the time are both evocative of nature (such as *Rain, Blue Rain, Wind*, or *Weather*) and laconically reflective (such as *Span, Days, Leaning In, Bracket,* or *Hours*). Her engagement with nature is elemental rather than bucolic, and the works shown also attest to her abiding painterly engagement with nature as envisaged by van Gogh, as well as Cézanne and Matisse. While her painting *Mountain* (1989, estate of Joan Mitchell) can be said to respond, in an abstract idiom, to Cézanne's almost obsessive images of *Mont Sainte-Victoire*, or while her thematizations of rain recall certain of van Gogh's images, such as *Rain* (1889, the Philadelphia Museum of Art), or *Landscape at Auvers in Rain* (1890, National Museum of Wales, Cardiff), her own method of working differed starkly from that of her predecessors. She never painted "before the motif," but rather in the seclusion of her studio and mostly under artificial illumination (although, as she admits to Michaud, she not only loves daylight but worries about the alterations of color effected by artificial light[46]). Her evocations of landscape and the elemental phenomena of nature are based chiefly on feeling, memory, and imaginative envisagement, as well as on the processes of mark-making themselves. She seeks to express essentiality rather than actuality. This aim may, to be sure, ultimately converge with that of her predecessors working figuratively in full view of nature, but this is an issue that requires a separate analysis. The question that poses itself here is how to understand Mitchell's quest for essentiality.

In the third chapter of *The Visible and the Invisible*, "Interrogation and Intuition," Merleau-Ponty is critical of both the philosophical search for pure essences (apprehended by intellectual intuition) and of an empirical immediacy unconcerned with essences; both are covert positivisms based ultimately on an understanding of truth as a coincidence between intellectual representation and reality. What is immediate, he reflects, "is at the horizon," and it is only "by remaining at a distance that it remains itself."[47] The distance is kept intact by the density of flesh, which is not an inert given, but rather, insofar as flesh is originary, it constitutes a bursting forth marked by noncoincidence and ceaseless differentiation.[48] In a Working Note of November 1959, Merleau-Ponty speaks of the 'World' (his quotation marks) as an ensemble within which every part, in its very singularity, opens up unlimited dimensions and becomes a "total part."[49] In its very singularity and partiality, he notes, a color, such as this yellow, can become "a universal or an element."[50]

Merleau-Ponty goes on, in chapter 4 of *The Visible and the Invisible*, titled "The Intertwining—the Chiasm," to describe and analyze idealities that cannot be thought meaningfully in detachment from sensory experience.[51] His examples, such as qualities of light or sound, the import of a single melodic phrase, or the apprehension of qualities such as bodily voluptuousness, closely follow Proust's studies in Swann's Way (Du côté de chez Swann), but in fact the idealities invoked are pervasive in the spectrum of experience. If they cannot truly be what they are except in being "veiled with shadows"[52] (so that they cannot aspire to the Cartesian ideal of clarity and distinctness), then neither can they be ascribed to the aesthetiological body in any reductive sense (which would contrast body with mind or spirit). As Merleau-Ponty puts it, they have their logic and their coherence, manifesting unknown "forces" and "laws" in their sensory presencing.[53] Furthermore, although he does not explicate this aspect of sensory presencing, they are also ethically significant in that they enable the development of empathy as well as an appreciation of the nonhuman world as being other than a mere resources at one's disposal (what Heidegger calls Bestand).

Genuine painting (as contrasted with skillful work that merely caters to a given configuration of the market[54]) has always appreciated the indissociability of visual appearances from connoted invisibles, or idealities. While this holds true of classical as well as modern figurative work, as well as of contemporary nonfigurative work, the latter can explore and communicate carnal essentialities without the distraction of narrative references and questions of explicable meaning.

Mitchell's essentialities are truly carnal, as well as marked by a pervasive sense of mortality and finitude (sometimes critically spoken of as her "morbidity," although in fact it attests to her heightened sensitivity and commitment to the raw truth of experience). While her diptych Mountain[55] signals a dialogue with Cézanne, no actual mountain is adumbrated by its agitated gestural strokes of blue, blue-black, Naples yellow, orange, and other hues, but rather the work gives expression to elemental earth, in its carnal essentiality, together with its rising toward and accommodating elemental water and air. Moreover, if the painter, in Merleau-Ponty's citation of Valéry, "brings his body to the task,"[56] this body is not just the empirical body nor yet the "body proper" that, with reference to Husserl, has long functioned as a translation of the German Leib in its distinction from Körper.[57] It is, rather, already expropriated rather than proper in the painter's self-forgetfulness that Mitchell emphasizes, without detriment to its carnality, as manifest in its gestures (and thus its expressive motility) as well as in both its afflictions and its resilience.

Mitchell usually titled her paintings after their completion, and in the 1989 Robert Miller Gallery show titles are frequently reused. A painting such as *Weather*[58] does not set out to capture or convey meteorological phenomena but rather, in its slashing and arcing deep-blue and grayed blue gestural strokes over a configuration of green, and with whites that seem to be both underlying and overpainted, it expresses one's carnal apprehension of and perilous exposure to the elemental turbulence of the atmosphere.

In the Working Note of November 1959, "The 'Senses'—Dimensionality—Being," Merleau-Ponty compares atonal music to painting "without the *skin* of things, but giving their flesh." He recognizes in both arts an equivalence to the thought of "the Being of indivision" (*l'Être d'indivision*).[59] Painting that renounces the "skin" of things renounces not only the identificatory superficiality of "profane vision" but also an ego or subject-centered preoccupation, on the part of the painter, with his or her identity and subjectivity. In a Working Note of April 1960, titled (in Greek letters, and with a reference to Homer) "*Ego* and *outis*" (Myself and nobody), Merleau-Ponty writes that the self (*Je*) is really no one and anonymous: "The first I (*le Je premier*), of which the nameable I is the objectification, is the unknown one to whom everything is given to see or to think."[60]

In contrast to the Sartrean negativity of consciousness understood as the "for-itself," which Merleau-Ponty discusses intensively and critically in the second chapter of *The Visible and the Invisible*, "Interrogation and Dialectic," the negativity of the anonymous self is "a negativity of openness, by the body, to the world."[61] This carnal openness, conjoined with a sensitivity making for unprotected exposure, is what allows for the self-forgetfulness that, for Mitchell, is integral to her creative process. It is what enables her to create paintings that, through painterly registers such as form, space, gestural calligraphy, and color, evoke and communicate essentialities that, being carnal, are nonetheless part and parcel of the invisibles indissociable from visual presencing. They are indissociable, furthermore, from both the parameters and the excesses of mortal experience.

Chapter 5

Plant Drawing, Abstraction, and the Philosophy of Nature

The Art of Ellsworth Kelly

> An image is nothing but an abstraction from the overwhelming deluge of sensations we experience.
>
> —Dore Ashton, catalogue essay in *Milton Avery: Mexico*

If Merleau-Ponty observed justly that the question of a choice between figuration and abstraction—a question that agitated art-theoretical discourse in the 1950s—was badly posed,[1] Ellsworth Kelly's art took the issue further: it undid or, one is tempted to say, deconstructed the supposed opposition. Although Kelly started out as an accomplished figurative painter, he already realized, upon his arrival in Paris in October 1948 (having completed army service from 1943 to 1945, followed by a course of study at Boston's Museum of Fine Arts), that figuration was not his path. During the six crucially formative years he spent in the city, he explored and nonfiguratively defamiliarized the visual aspects of the architecture and everyday environment of Paris; but an important turning point occurred in 1949 when, having purchased a potted hyacinth in bloom, he proceeded to draw it in ink in sparse contour line, with its form rising from the lower margin of the format and being truncated by its top.[2] The drawing is nonmimetic in renouncing any three-dimensional make-believe by shading or other modeling, as well as color, and it also disregards conventional floral attractiveness. However, it presents the very essence of the plant in showing its sturdy vegetative fleshiness conjoined with the elegance of its reflexed, bell-shaped blooms. There ensued further drawings, in pencil or ink, of plant forms, notably strings of seaweed and pine branches, translated into pure linear rhythms or, more rarely, into silhouette. These works had an ancestry in Kelly's drawings of trees during and immediately after his wartime military service and, more remotely, in his childhood engagement with nature and particularly his fascination with the ornithological paintings of John James Audubon. Astonishing as it may seem, it was, in particular, the seaweed and hyacinth drawings that opened up his path to abstraction. To quote his own words: "The drawings from plant life seem to be the bridge to the way of seeing that brought about the paintings in 1949 that are the basis for all my later work."[3]

How is one to understand this way of seeing? It is one that, in breaking with what Merleau-Ponty calls profane vision, rejects the subject-object dichotomy that ordinary vision presupposes, due to being geared, as it is, to identification and to pursuit or avoidance Kelly sought, in particular, to steer clear of both the cult of the artist's subjectivity or personality and of the prosaic objectivity of culturally sanctioned meanings. Only by effacing such meanings could vision truly come into its own, allowing what is seen to come to presence in its (nonconceptual) essentiality (an essentiality akin to Heidegger's verbally, rather than substantively, based understanding of essence as *wesen*).[4] In much the same spirit, Merleau-Ponty quotes Robert Delaunay's remark that the world is "according to my perspective, *so as to be* independent of me, which is for me *so as to be* without me, to be world."[5]

If the profane (in the Latin sense of the ordinary) connotes sacrality as its counterpart, the latter involves, in visual art, the visual quale's opening unto its proper invisibles or, in Merleau-Ponty's words, to manifest "a lining of the invisible in the strict sense, which it renders present as a certain absence."[6] In contrast to form that is readily identifiable, and to essences grasped in static self-identity, by a purely mental apprehension, such presencings of absence can evoke the genuine essentiality of plant forms, such as Kelly's hyacinth. Kelly himself has spoken of (nonmimetically) wanting to capture in his work the elusiveness or mystery of visible reality.[7]

Practices of Plant Drawing

Echoing Merleau-Ponty's reflection, in "Eye and Mind," that the historicity of painting advances not straightforwardly but "by detours, transgression, encroachment, and sudden breakthroughs,"[8] Robert Storr notes that an artist's eventual assimilation and transformation of the influences of her formative years, or her ability to grasp the full bearing of her own innovative achievements, are unpredictable aspects of the creative process. Furthermore, "such leaps and lags are the hallmark of authentic artistic identity, the choices that render a given artist's work unique."[9]

Among Kelly's significant early influences, Storr singles out, along with Picasso, the German expressionist painter Max Beckmann; and it was Beckmann who declared, in his Boston lecture of 1948 (which Kelly attended), that "one must have the deepest respect for what the eye sees."[10] For Kelly, such respect came to mean that the well-spring of his mature and resolutely nonmimetic art remained concretely "what the eye sees" in its constant investigation of the visible world. Kelly's interlinking of an autonomous formal vocabulary with a fine-tuned visual investigation of concrete appearances was fundamentally what enabled him to undo the supposed opposition between reference to reality and pure abstraction. "In my paintings," he states with characteristic directness and lucidity, "I am not inventing; my ideas come from constantly investigating how things look."[11] As late as 2006, he still declared that, although his work was never expressionist, "Beckmann's visual force has informed my painting."[12] This relentless investigation of vision and visibility is what links his art to Merleau-Ponty's thought perhaps as closely as Cézanne's (even though the philosopher, deeply attentive as he was to Cézanne, took no notice of Kelly, in keeping with the latter's early nonrecognition or incomprehension in France). If Kelly's practice of plant drawing was integral to his meditation on "what the eye sees" and was thus obedient to Beckmann's exhortation, Picasso's acknowledged and relevant inspiration may have been the exquisite quality of line in many of his drawings or etchings (which Kelly is known to have admired).

It was thus not Kelly's but rather Matisse's free and lyrical line, inspired by the arabesque and described by the artist himself as "enlivening" (*vivifiante*[13]), that particularly enchanted Merleau-Ponty (who included a Matisse line drawing of a woman bather in the image file of "Eye and Mind"). In the 1930s and beyond, Matisse, like Kelly, kept up a practice of plant drawing. For Kelly, but emphatically not for Matisse, plant motifs remain strictly confined to his graphic work. Matisse, furthermore, sometimes used volumetric shading in his botanical drawings, and he also included contextual elements such as vases, flowerpots, or decorative motifs. In contrast, Kelly's plant drawings remain strictly and sparsely linear (excepting the occasional silhouette and a very few works in colored ink or watercolor), and devoid of context. Both Kelly's and Matisse's plant drawings essentialize botanical forms, and for both the essentiality of plants in their visual and sensuous presencing is intuitively apprehended, obviating any need for mimetic representation. As Eric de Chassey observes, Matisse privileges a unitary or holistic apprehension of form, suffused with feeling, whereas Kelly's graphic trait tends, in its purifying essentialization, toward an initial fragmentation and isolation of forms, which is then surmounted by a "mysterious synthesis."[14]

After a hiatus of nearly eight years following 1949, and thus spanning his return to the United States in 1954, Kelly resumed his practice of plant drawing, maintaining, in Axsom's words, "his commitment to refreshing his vision in direct contact with nature through drawing."[15] Photographs of his Manhattan studios on Broad Street and later on Coenties Slip show a collection of potted foliage plants, while sunflowers as well as corn flourished in pots on the roof at Coenties Slip. He did not, however, begin formally to show his plant drawings until 1969.[16]

Having already created his first lithographs in France in 1949, Kelly began a sustained practice of printmaking in 1964, in the course of which he created several series of plant lithographs. These series, such as *Twelve Leaves* (1978), or *Series of Oak Leaves* (1992), allow for an enhanced impact of pure line and form in space by their substantive formats, and by the value (brightness) contrast between the inked line and Kelly's usual choice of bright white (mostly Arches) paper.[17] His preferred technique was the indirect method of transfer lithography (in which the lithographic crayon drawing is executed on transfer paper or mylar, rather than directly on a lithographic stone or a metal plate), allowing him to bypass the distorting reversal of the image required by the traditional direct method.[18]

For exploring Kelly's visual meditations on vegetal form in their relation to Merleau-Ponty's thought, two thematic foci suggest themselves: first, the interrelation of eye and mind, or rather eye, mind, and hand; and, second, the complex involvement of memory.

As Axsom notes, Kelly already honed his extraordinary ability "to integrate eye, mind, and hand" by his practice, in 1949–1950, of drawing with his eyes closed—not in a surrealist quest to free the unconscious but rather so as to disengage his drawing from representation and to work from visual memory.[19] Merleau-Ponty writes that the painter is sovereign in his exploration of the world "without any other 'technique' than the spontaneous one that his eyes and hands give themselves in virtue of seeing, in virtue of painting."[20] His own sustained interrogation of Descartes's *Optics*, confronted with his analyses of painting, leads him to argue that vision cannot be understood (as Descartes understood it) as an essentially mental operation, interpretively relying on bodily indices, and in the framework of a subject-object schema. A philosophical interrogation of painting reveals instead that she who sees "is immersed within the visible by her body, itself visible," so that ultimately there is no defined boundary between seer and seen.[21] Visual qualities are given only insofar as they evoke, within the body, a "carnal formula" of their presencing, enabling the artist's hand to call forth a visible trace or "icon" thereof that enables and invites others to see "in accordance with it."[22]

Kelly's plant drawings are consonant with, but also amplify, Merleau-Ponty's analyses. As Axsom notes, his linear gestures convey "the energy and speed of their execution."[23] Their execution involves, as Axsom further observes, the full range of motion of Kelly's arm (certainly in the lithographs, given their size), while his eyes remain focused on the plant before him and not on his drawing in progress, until its creation is accomplished.[24] Kelly works swiftly by what he calls a "searching line," which seeks the vegetal motif's essential form. The bond between eye and hand (which is at least as intimate for artists as the bond of either to mind) is thus not a spontaneous given (as Merleau-Ponty seems to understand it) but rather an achievement that requires effort to inactivate prosaic recognition, commonplace meanings, and the prominence of the self. Axsom acknowledges that his comments on Kelly's process suggest a kinship on its part to Chinese and Japanese calligraphy. While also requiring that energy pass from the artist's entire arm and body to the hand, ideographic calligraphy allows the viewer to follow the order and execution of strokes, which is, however, mandated here by ideographic tradition, rather than being, as for Kelly, a free response to the living and mutable botanical form.

Since, for Merleau-Ponty, visual presencing brings into play a complexity of invisibles (which are such de jure, and not merely de facto), it is everywhere informed by "participations" that are indissociable from memory. Even a supposed mere sense datum, such as a patch of red, reveals itself upon analysis to be "a knot within the weft of the simultaneous and the successive," or a "momentary crystallization" of visibility, informed throughout by both imagination and memory.[25] Kelly's work, as Gavin Delahunty notes, attests constantly to these rich depth strata of visual perception, amalgamating observation with diacritical articulations as well as with memory.[26] Axsom attests to the variability of Kelly's process in creating his plant lithographs: Kelly may (in keeping with his well-known practice of revisiting and "interpreting" his earlier sketches, drawings, or collages) carry forward drawings whose primary function was "finding form," or else recreate accomplished drawings (but without ever reproducing them). Finally, he may draw purely from memory (as he does with the simple form of *Catalpa Leaf*), or he may freely draw plant forms on transfer paper with no reference to anything preexisting in his graphic work, as in his *Series of Plant and Flower Lithographs* (1984–1985).[27] This sheer variability of process attests to the density of the field within which perceptual experience articulates and communicates itself, a density that is ultimately indissociable from memory.

Edge, Line, and Space

Kelly's 1951 painting *Colors for a Large Wall*[28] consists of sixty-four square, conjoined, and individually monochrome canvas panels, marking his engagement, at the time, with the grid, as well as with chance (which informs the color sequences). Both are antithetical to traditional canons of composition, which Kelly was determined to avoid. Concerning his decision to conjoin separate stretched canvases, rather than painting the sixty-four squares on a single canvas, he comments: "I wanted an edge for each color, I wanted it to begin and to end, so that it had its own uniqueness. . . . [I]n the world, every object / form has its edges . . . *I didn't want to depict*. In order not to depict, I had to make the panels."[29] The separative edges (together with the flat or unmodulated, and thus depersonalized, application of paint) constituted, for Kelly, an antidote to both mimetic depiction and to a subjective statement, thus allowing the work to function on its own, and often in vital interchange with architectural space, rather than being just a picture to hang on a wall.

If the dividing line between panels nonetheless falls short of actual edges in defining form, its linearity also cannot be straightforwardly eliminated by joining monochrome panels, since their conjoined edges themselves create lines (even though these lines can hardly be called depictive and do not convey the energy of the artist's trait[30]). In 1953, Kelly created his first *Spectrum* painting, which followed the spectrum's progression of hues, circling from yellow back to yellow within a single canvas divided into fourteen vertical sections[31] whose demarcated edges could hardly avoid remaining "depictive." In the mid-1960s, Kelly resumed working with multiple monochrome panels (having previously explored, after his return to the United States, what Paik aptly calls a figure/ground mode, as well as curvilinear shapes in both his painting and planar abstract sculptures).[32] He returned to his fascination with the spectrum in three multi-panel works of 1966–1967. Concerning the first of these, *Spectrum II*, Paik comments that "it forms a large vertical polyptych, the first of its kind in scale as well as in number of panels [there are thirteen] . . . set side by side."[33]

It was only with his magnificent *Spectrum V* of 1969, however, that Kelly chose to separate the panels by actual intervals of blank wall, avoiding linear definition entirely and giving each panel its autonomous presence, set off against (and edged in by) a neutral whiteness, yet communicating, through form and hue, across the interstices with the remaining ones.[34]

Even from this selective vantage point on Kelly's abstract main body of work, and perhaps specifically as concerns the issues of line and edge, one may well ask what Kelly's long-sustained practice of plant drawing may have contributed to his central creative endeavor. Was it perhaps in the end mainly a private passion or indulgence? It maintained, to be sure, a pure and austere linearity that was shared by the artist's occasional portrait drawings (including an exquisite drawing of his longtime partner Jack Shear), and that in no way privileged edges over descriptive or figurative line. Rather, it allowed the contour line on its own to define spatiality and perspective as well as expressive relationships.

Merleau-Ponty characterizes the line, released at last, within Western art, to be "neither an intimation of things nor a thing," but to deploy itself in its own right as "a certain disequilibrium" or as a charge of energy disrupting "the indifference of the white paper," and ultimately as "a certain erosion practiced within the in-itself."[35] His entire fine-tuned characterization could readily, and even in an exemplary fashion, be applied to Kelly's line in his plant drawings. Merleau-Ponty (who never engaged with Kelly's art) applies it nonetheless chiefly to Klee's and Matisse's line and does not confront the difficult question of what such a line's relationship is to edges or to art that, while not renouncing a quest for essentiality, seeks to break with depiction.

To say that Kelly's plant drawings refreshed his vision in contact with nature is not enough. At the least, they also sensitized it in a way that the diverse, humanly created structures within which he found, and from which he extracted, pictorial forms, could not. He did, to be sure, not refer to plant forms in his nonfigurative work in the way that he did refer explicitly to "already made" forms, such as the arch of a bridge and its reflection (see *White Plaque* of 1955), or to forms created by shadow patterns cast by and upon an outdoor metal staircase, nor even by moving shadows cast upon an open book in the course of a bus ride.[36] These are aspects of what one might call a purely visual (rather than ideal) constitution that, as Merleau-Ponty observes (with allusion to one of Cézanne's paintings of *Mont Sainte-Victoire*), remain commonly unperceived.[37] Given that the question of how Kelly's practice of plant drawing may have informed his artistic vision remains still largely unexplored, it will here be treated, in an initial manner, chiefly along two avenues: the sensitization of vision to both line and edge by natural forms, and to what are traditionally called positive and negative spaces (or form and interval) together with its involvement of memory and expression.

Kelly characterizes his plant drawings as an impersonal observation of botanical form.[38] Such "impersonal" devotion to the way in which a living organism manifests itself as a linear configuration, articulated within a given pictorial format, and irrespective of anyone's artistic predilections, cannot fail to sensitize vision to the self-deployment of line or edge in space. The fact that Kelly, in the cited text, states that Matisse was not among his inspirations during his years in France,[39] playing no part in Kelly's inception of his plant drawings (despite later efforts to highlight relationships between the two artists) may indicate an important difference already adumbrated: Matisse's approach takes plant life up into a personal, sensuous, and expressive vision, whereas Kelly's seeks to be "impersonally" faithful to its self-manifestation.

It is not surprising that one can perceive an echo of the sensuous linearity of some of Kelly's plant-based lithographs, such as "Melon Leaf" or "Pear," in the curvilinear forms subtly articulated within his nonfigurative paintings such as *Black Ripe* or *Red Blue*.[40] Kelly's first major abstract sculpture, *Sculpture for a Large Wall* of 1957 (initially created for the lobby of the Transportation Building at Penn Center, Philadelphia),[41] shows, as Paik observes, "more subtle curves than he had been making at the time." She quotes his own comment that (notwithstanding careful planning) the execution of this work was "like a trance; my curves came at the right time. It was like writing."[42] The allusions to trance and to writing bring to mind Axsom's comment that, in Kelly's plant lithographs, "orchestration of shape, weight, and balance occur spontaneously, while he is drawing," without either calculation or revision.[43] This characterization recalls the Zen practice of brush drawing the *enzo*, or circle shape (and Kelly was well acquainted with Asian calligraphic traditions from his student days at Boston's Museum of Fine Arts, with its extensive Asian collection). His meditative and sustained close attention to botanical forms may be at least partly credited for the consummate spontaneity of his own abstract curvilinear forms, and even perhaps for the subtle way in which his totem sculptures, which he

Plant Drawing, Abstraction, and the Philosophy of Nature   83

began to make in the mid-1970s, interlink, in their edges, the articulations of the concave and convex with both groundedness and soaring verticality.⁴⁴ "In my painting," Kelly states, "negative space is never arbitrary."⁴⁵ It is integral to the work as a whole, rather than forming a more or less neutral ground for a configuration in focus. Implicit in the idea of a purely and arbitrarily negative space is the Cartesian understanding of space as geometric extension, which Merleau-Ponty characterizes in "Eye and Mind":

> Space [thus understood] is in-itself, or rather it is the in-itself *par excellence*, its definition is to be in-itself. Each point of space is, and is thought [as being] right where it is, one here, the other there; space is the self-evidence of the where. Orientation, polarity, envelopment are, within it, derivative phenomena . . .⁴⁶

This philosophical absolutization of space that Merleau-Ponty characterizes and criticizes (while nevertheless acknowledging its salutary import at a certain juncture of intellectual history) is inimical to ambiguity, which Kelly's art, by contrast, richly explores. Commenting, for example, on Kelly's 1954 painting, *Black Curves*,⁴⁷ Delahunty notes that its two identical black forms, placed one above the other, "are somehow both an instrument to draw our attention to the white ground and autonomous entities possessing a definite power over the painting."⁴⁸ He also quotes Henry Geldzahler's observation that, in Kelly's work, "what read at first as clear and simple forms rapidly become ambiguous and remain ambiguous."⁴⁹ Given the flattening of botanical form as well as the autonomy of line in Kelly's plant drawings and lithographs, they constitute an ample resource for a visual meditation on spatial ambiguity and complexity, and ultimately on the inextricability of positive and negative space. To point out just two examples: in *Cyclamen V* and *X* (in Kelly's *Suite of Plant Lithographs*), the linear intricacies of stems and petals obviate any definite distinction between plant forms and the void spaces they circumscribe; and in *Oak VI* (in *Series of Oak Leaves*), the dented, overlapping leaves create linear rhythms and spatial complexities irrespective of any facile distinction between figure and ground.

One could also study Kelly's scattering of isolated foliar forms, such as those of grape leaves or acanthus, and the tensional unity in which, despite their scattering, they remain poised, in relation to the coherence of the dispersed monochrome panels in some of Kelly's late work that fuses painting with architecture. Gary Garrels thus describes his work for the LVMH Forum Auditorium in Paris (in a museum complex designed by Frank Gehry) as being, like the building's interior, "fragmented and dynamic, fragments or whole panels [of which there are six of different sizes and colors that] appear and disappear as one moves through the space."[50] Merleau-Ponty is sensitive to such complexity and reflects that, for this reason, a painter's vision can realize itself only through sustained study and work.[51] Although his discussion remains focused on traditional easel painting and does not envisage interlinking it with the mural-size works of abstract expressionism, nor with painting that is integral to architecture, he does comment on the "system of equivalences" that makes such interlinkings possible in the first place.[52]

Kelly's long-cherished project of creating a building whose architecture was entirely his own, and which would display some of his paintings and sculpture, could not be fully realized during his lifetime (due to problems that arose with an original commission in Santa Barbara, California). However, the building (or secular chapel, as it has been called) has now been constructed on the campus of the University of Texas at Austin, and *Austin*, as the work is called, promises to become a center of artistic pilgrimage. Colored glass in different configurations, in place of the building's windows, casts the radiant hues of the spectrum on granite and marble, and one of Kelly's totem sculptures rises in what could be called the sanctum. It was to be, Kelly said, a place to rest one's eyes and mind.[53] Although much more modest in scale and complexity, his plant drawings (which number in the thousands) offer a similar respite and repose.

Excursus: Plant Drawing in the Context of Botanical Art

To look at Kelly's plant drawings and lithographs today is to see them in their double relation to contemporary nonfigurative art as well as to the recent renaissance of botanical art. This renaissance builds upon a long historical tradition initiated in Europe but now spanning the Americas, as well as China, Japan, South Korea, South Africa, and Australia. Although Merleau-Ponty mentions plant drawing or botanical painting only twice in "Eye and Mind,"[54] and not at all in his other aesthetic writings, he does present it as showing that figuration and abstraction are not only inextricable, but that they also converge if pursued to their extremes, so that, for instance, a study by Klee of two holly leaves makes them appear monstrous or surreal by the very exactitude of their rendering; whereas, in contrast, and even though perhaps no real cluster of grapes ever looked like Caravaggio's grapes, these painted images are "the grape itself."[55]

Caravaggio's grapes function in the contexts of various early still lifes that themselves often constitute part of more complex paintings. Although the tradition of still life painting may historically have impeded the autonomy of botanical art, this autonomy has asserted itself since at least the fifteenth and early sixteenth centuries, when Albrecht Dürer (1471–1528) painted exquisite studies of roadside grasses and weeds, and Leonardo da Vinci (1452–1519) drew the wild flora of Tuscany for its own sake, with no ulterior purpose of illustration or decoration.[56] From the seventeenth century on until botanical art was temporarily eclipsed by the development of color photography in the early twentieth century, these artists were followed, in the botanical domain, by luminaries such as Maria Sibylla Merian (1647–1717), Georg Dionysius Ehret (1708–1770), Ferdinand Bauer (1760–1826), and the brothers Pierre-Joseph and Henri-Joseph Redouté (respectively, 1759–1840 and 1768–1857).

Kelly himself echoes these artists' devotion to the study of nature when he recalls that, as a child, he spent all his spare time looking at birds and insects (beetles). He comments: "my 'color use' and the object quality of the 'painting,' and the use of fragmentation is closer to birds and beetles and fish than to de Stijl and Constructivism."[57]

It is, of course, remarkable for a major and highly innovative contemporary nonfigurative artist to trace his abiding formative influences not to art history (which now often reveals its heritage of colonialism and cultural appropriation), but to a lifelong study of natural forms. Kelly had in fact also taken up bird watching at a young age, and while his mature work is appreciated for paring down form and color to their essential purity, his early fascination was with the ornithological paintings of Audubon.

The recent renaissance of botanical art owes a major debt to botanist and collector Shirley Sherwood, who began collecting botanical art on an extensive and international scale in the 1990s, and who has enhanced its visibility and standards of excellence through exhibitions, books, and sponsorship of educational ventures. Sherwood distinguishes between two main motivational currents in the renaissance of botanical art, each of which she associates with a guiding artist.[58] One of these artists, Margaret Mee (1909–1988), was a pioneering and daring explorer of the flora of Amazonia, documenting it in her compelling paintings and calling attention to the urgent need for conservation. The other artist, Rory McEwen (1932–1980), sought to engage, in large part through his botanical work (executed in watercolor on vellum), in dialogue with developments in contemporary art. He eventually abandoned a career in music for his visual art and created, besides botanical paintings, etchings, collage, and sculpture in glass and other translucent media. Perhaps his culminating achievement is his 1978–1981 series of paintings of single leaves, often autumnal and sometimes disintegrating, set into expanses of blank space.[59]

Kelly's practice of plant drawing (which, like Matisse's, preceded in its inception the renaissance of botanical art) is autonomous. Botanical art pursues and must pursue verisimilitude, which it achieves not only through exactitude of observation, but also by the use of perspective (including aerial perspective), modeling, and techniques to convey the pliancy or stiffness, as well as the texture of plants in their visual relation to light. Ideally, of course, its illusory evocation of plant forms evokes both their three-dimensional actuality and their essentiality and offers also an aesthetically compelling image. In contrast, Kelly's linear plant drawings, accomplished without erasure or other correction, renounces illusory verisimilitude in favor of deploying the energies of line, form, and space in their own right. They create an effect not of three-dimensional tangibility but of what Axsom calls "transparency": a desolidification that also connotes the transience or ephemerality of both presencing and representation. Nonetheless, and despite Kelly's habitual flattening of forms, the third dimension as well as perspectival relationships are evoked without being explicitly asserted, due to the focus of his gaze and the sensitivity of his line. One unmistakably encounters, for instance, the weightiness of fruit, the papery dryness of a daffodil's calyx, or the intricate and fragile plication of a sweet pea flower. As Rémi Labrusse comments, it is not the artist here who comes upon his motif but the phenomena that come toward him.[60] They do so, to cite Labrusse once more, "in their unshakeable ipseity," exceeding verisimilitude.[61] Merleau-Ponty ultimately traces such events of encounter to the reversibility (without coincidence) between seer and seen (rejecting, once again, the subject-object dichotomy). He understands the line that bodies forth a natural entity as one that, for Klee, "renders visible," or that constitutes, for Leonardo, the "generative axis" of a living form.[62]

In contradistinction to botanical art, Kelly does not seek pleasingly to compose the plant forms within the pictorial format, but rather lets them emerge, in an often surprising manner, through the effraction of space by line. This is one respect in which his plant drawings or lithographs are comparable, for all the difference between their sheer linearity and McEwen's paintings on vellum, to the latter's late series of single leaves. Though placed within vast expanses of space, these leaves may occupy just a corner of the format (as though they had drifted there) or be truncated by its edges. Space shows itself to be primordial and thus anterior to cultural constructs, and as being integral to what Merleau-Ponty speaks of as the basis of "inhuman nature" on which such constructs have established themselves.[63]

Plant-Being, Plant Drawing, and the Philosophy of Nature

In his three lecture courses on Nature,[64] Merleau-Ponty maintains an unbroken silence concerning plants, even though plants constitute well over three-quarters of the earth's biomass, and even though animal life would be largely impossible without the extraordinary ability of plants to take nourishment directly from the solar energy by means of photosynthesis, to say nothing of the complex evolutionary interrelationships between animals and plants. Merleau-Ponty's oblivion of plants may, in part, reflect his preoccupation with behavior, ranging from his early work, *The Structure of Behavior*, to his assertion, voiced in his second Nature course in response to George E. Coghill's researches on the embryonic development and maturation of the axolotl lizard (*Amblystoma tigrinum*), that "the emergence of behavior and the maturation of the organism are one and the same thing."[65]

It might seem that, in the case of organisms largely incapable of locomotion, such as plants, one cannot meaningfully speak of behavior; yet Merleau-Ponty himself includes sessile animals, such as sea anemones or certain marine worms, in his discussion of animal behavior. He points out that behavior is a biological concept in-process of transformation, and the transformations that are of particular interest to him concern the very notions of behavior and that of information and communication.[66]

While plants lack brains, neurons, or a nervous system, these bases of sensitivity or consciousness are, as Merleau-Ponty notes, not ultimately explanatory of animal behavior, given that it emerges from a pre-neural dynamics.[67] In plants, such a dynamics is not pre-neural but non-neural, and largely chemical in nature, issuing in an array of chemically based plant senses to which humans have only limited access. Hence, even in the context of a Merleau-Pontian primacy of perception, plant perception remains largely disregarded. Nevertheless, plants evidently sense and respond optimally for purposes of survival (including species survival) to a spectrum of environmental conditions, including (but not limited to) different wavelengths or intensities and comparative durations of light, soil structure, moisture, the presence of chemicals, microbes, insects, and larger herbivores, as well as disturbance or even mere touch, which can, for instance, prompt the release of protective volatile oils or poisonous compounds. Plants also respond to electrical or chemical signals from other plants, transmitted either through the air or, more efficiently, through the vast underground mycorrhizal network. Interconnected response is a reason why plant behavior has, as naturalist Michael Pollan notes, been compared to "swarm behavior" in social insects, such as ants or bees.[68] It hardly needs pointing out that plants, by virtue of their chemical ingenuity, compensate for the disadvantages of their sessile mode of life by producing a plethora of survival-enhancing pharmaceuticals, nutrients, scents attractive to pollinators, and poisons. In a recent article, Patricia Locke argues that even microbial life, and in particular the human (and animal) microbiomes, "meet (although obviously in a limited way) the criteria for perception, cognition, and intentional movement that we attribute to a sense of self."[69] Leaving out of consideration here questions as to the attribution of conscious awareness or a sense of self to microorganisms and to plants (which are highly complex and sophisticated organisms), it is imperative to extend the Merleau-Pontian philosophical interpretation of the mid-twentieth-century "new biology" from his own exclusive focus on animal life to encompass vegetal and perhaps even microbial life.

In plants, as in animals, aesthetic creativity far exceeds functional utility. Flowering plants in particular, and their zoological partners, engage in it as though in a mutuality of play or dance. Given the chemical basis of plant perception and communication, this creativity does not only take visual form (the auditory being generally marginal) but is often olfactory. Functionality may certainly be dominant, as in the stenches (to human sensibility) that some inflorescences emit so as to attract flies as their pollinators, but exquisite perfumes likewise abound (and are often emitted during the hours of day or night when specific pollinators are active). Thus, for instance, the beautiful euglossine bees that pollinate the Brazil nut tree are dependent for their reproduction, and thus their existence as a species, on orchid fragrances, which the male bee harvests so as to create from them his own perfume, which is an indispensable courtship enticement. If, as Merleau-Ponty writes, animal copulation "is essentially the establishment of an action of presence,"[70] such expressive action is not limited to the animal kingdom but is no less prominent in the vegetal domain.

Given the reality of plant perception and of the fine-tuned responsiveness of plants to environmental stimuli, the question arises whether one could speak of plants having their own *Umwelt* (surrounding world) forming a structure of relevance for the organism and a framework for actional response. In plants, such response tends to be commonly unperceived by human observers, since it is often concentrated at the subterranean level of roots. Jakob von Uexküll (1864–1984), founder of *Umwelt* theory, does not hesitate to ascribe *Umwelten* to the lowly invertebrates with which he chiefly worked. Merleau-Ponty reflects that, even though such living beings "work only with physico-chemical elements," these are taken up into "a milieu of events."[71] In animals, he speaks of their developing "an architectonic of symbols," so that the *Umwelt* finally becomes less and less teleological in favor of being oriented toward the interpretation of symbols.[72] One then needs to question whether any such architectonic of symbols might even be prefigured in the vegetal domain. If one considers the complexities of coevolutionary relationships between plants and animals, it certainly becomes questionable on what basis one could restrict *Umwelt* to the zoological partner and deny it to the botanical one. For instance, the male and female of a single species of hummingbird, the purple-throated carib (*Eulampis jugularis*), are dimorphic and have evolved anatomical differences that allow them to take nectar from, and pollinate, different species of *Heliconia* (*H. bihai* and *H. caribea*). In this reciprocity of male and female bird anatomy and of species-specific flower structure, an elaboration of *Umwelten* seems to come into play that is irrespective of the customary division between plant and animal. An even more striking example is the fine-tuned adaptations of certain flowering plants to bats as pollinators, which involves their dealing, in strategic ways, with the intricacies of echolocation.[73] Although the question of plant *Umwelten* can only be raised and not exhaustively discussed or answered here, raising it is an important corrective to Heidegger's restriction of *Umwelt* (a notion for which he is indebted to Uexküll) to *Da-sein*, declaring animals to be "poor in world," and mineral nature to lack it, while rarely making even the most cursory reference to plants.[74]

In a meditation on Whitehead's concept of nature, focused on time, space, and events, Merleau-Ponty reflects that "nature" is comparable to the being of a wave, the reality of which is only global and not fragmentary.[75] It is then not possible to think of the world as composed of "punctual spatio-temporal existences,"[76] and fragmenting divisions drawn within nature become blurred or "ragged." Since nature, moreover, is "that in which we are" and so cannot be contemplated with the distancing gaze of a *kosmotheoros*, Merleau-Ponty finds that substantialist thinking is not defensible.[77] Bernhard Waldenfels notes further that the chiastic structure, for Merleau-Ponty, of being-in or of *Ineinander* is marked by dissymmetry: "A chiasm that is able to give symbolic expression to what takes place between us and the things, between me and others, should be thought of as an asymmetrical and irreversible Ineinander."[78] A lateral *Ineinander*, as Merleau-Ponty calls it, is characteristic not only of the interrelations of humanity with animality but is pervasive within nature and thus cannot fail to embrace the being of plants.

It might seem to be a stretch to return from these reflections on the philosophy of nature to Kelly's plant drawings, but this impression is misleading. Kelly's pencil, ink, and lithographic plant drawings allow natural forms to arise and manifest themselves in their powerful yet insubstantial essentiality. Their sparse contour linearity frees them from the habitualities of profane vision, as well as from mimetic aspirations and decorative trivialization. They are also disengaged from the artist's subjectivity, since his gaze is unselfconsciously absorbed in the autonomous articulation of botanical forms and is also at one with his drawing gestures and medium. The drawings convey what Merleau-Ponty likes to call the nonpositive character of manifestation by an effect of transparency stemming not only from their pure and sensitive linearity, but also from the envelopment of form in space together with its penetration by space. Far from the plants or parts of plants shown being isolated fragments of the world, their drawn forms' searching, yet intuitively assured linear rhythms recall Merleau-Ponty's comparison (with reference to Whitehead) of the presencing of nature to the being of a wave. The rhythm of the wave holds sway over whatever is swept along, and it also constitutes a late echo of what Anaximander's one surviving fragment calls the *taxis* or ordering of time.[79] It may at times call into question the clarity of a form's demarcation from other forms, as in Kelly's 1986 drawing *Burdock*, in which the edge of the main leaf shape also forms the fragmentary contour of another.[80] The seriality that Kelly cultivates in his plant drawings, either by their thematic arrangement or by slowly turning part of a plant held in one hand, such as the inflorescence of a calla lily, as he draws its changing perspectival aspects. Time is, of course, the very core of transience and ephemerality that erodes natural forms not only by the inevitable despoilment that follows upon their flourishing, but also in their coming to presence and their flourishing itself. Through these aspects, Kelly's plant drawings offer a visual antidote to the entrenched habits of reification and substantialist thinking with regard to nature.

Kelly's practice of seeing rejects what Merleau-Ponty characterizes as "profane vision" as well as mimesis in favor of a purifying essentialization that consummately organizes form, line, and space. It integrates observation with memory and differential articulation. Kelly's career-long practice of plant-drawing allowed for the development of an autonomous line (such as Merleau-Ponty discusses in "Eye and Mind"), as well as Kelly's sensitivity to edges, and his rejection of any merely negative, quasi-Cartesian space.

Although the contemporary renaissance of botanical art has tended toward artistic inventiveness and abstraction, it remains by its nature committed to verisimilitude, in contrast to the "transparency" of Kelly's plant drawings, which conveys what Merleau-Ponty speaks of as the nonpositive character of manifestation. It is today no longer defensible to deny the existence of plant behavior (despite, as already noted, plants' sessile mode of life and their lack of a nervous system). It may become desirable, nonetheless, to credit them with an *Umwelt* or species-specific world articulation, and certainly artistic practices such as Kelly's facilitate renouncing habits of thought that fall short of the complexities and richness of reality.

Chapter 6

Strong Beauty and Structures of Exclusion

> The work of art effects an upheaval of the transcendental illusion and its acceptance of the given purely as such . . . and thinks from before the thought that tends toward absolutization and totalization.
>
> —Rajiv Kaushik, *Art, Language and Figure in Merleau-Ponty: Excursions in Hyper-Dialectic*

The critique and eclipse of beauty as an artistic aim and ideal, prominent since the early twentieth century, is interlinked with what Jean-Luc Nancy speaks of as "the magnitude and intensity of the transformations to which the history of art has exposed us within a single century."[1] This single century spans, for him, roughly from 1850 to 1950, so that "it cuts across Auschwitz" and other genocidal events of the twentieth century. On a global scale, such events did not, of course, reach a point of exhaustion by midcentury (one need only recall Cambodia, Tibet, and Rwanda), nor of course has there been any more recent dearth of radical innovation in the arts. It may rather be that the eclipse of beauty that became prominent in midcentury art and art-theoretical discourse—whether in favor of an exaltation of sublimity over beauty's seeming irrelevance or affront to the state of the world or, more generally, of "content" over "aesthetics," reflects

---

An initial version of this chapter was presented as an invited lecture at the 2019 conference of the International Merleau-Ponty Circle at Brock University, Canada, under the direction of Rajiv Kaushik. It was recently published in Emmanuel Alloa, Frank Choraqui, and Rajiv Kaushik, eds., *Merleau-Ponty and Contemporary Philosophy* (Albany: State University of New York Press, 2019), 281–296.

also an awareness of its possible, and actualized, complicity with evil. One thinks here of what Nancy characterizes as Nazism's, and specifically Hitler's, quest for a worldview that would galvanize the masses, being "placed before [their] eyes and given presence in its totality, its [supposed] truth, and its destiny."[2] The artist who paradigmatically accomplished this sort of (re)presentational mandate is, of course, Leni Riefenstahl who, to the end of her long life, named beauty as the sole aim and absolute value of her work in film and photography—an aim that supposedly left her blameless for the spectacular success of her Nazi propaganda. To cite Nancy once more, the vision that Nazism advocated is one that repudiates any sort of "withdrawn invisibility."[3] As such, it is antithetical to Merleau-Ponty's thought of the intricate inter-involvement of visibility with invisibles; and the contrast highlights the political relevance of his ontologically oriented late thought.

In *The Retrieval of the Beautiful*, Galen Johnson points out the long-standing confusion of beauty with hierarchies of perfection that lend themselves to the idolization of ideological, racist, sexist, and other prejudices.[4] Even Heidegger, in *Besinnung* of 1938, satirizes the National Socialist ideal of male beauty and comments memorably that beauty functions here as "what pleases and must please the power-essence [*dem Machtwesen*] of the beast of prey, man."[5] In "The Misadventures of Beauty," Neal Benezra discusses an image of the 1937 bronze sculpture *Readiness* by Arno Breker, an artist acclaimed by National Socialism.[6] It evinces both a reappropriation of classical Greek ideals (notably as embodied in the work of Polykleitos) and, as Benezra points out, an utter and startling (as well as non-Greek) lack of sensuousness. This lack has an echo in Heidegger's sensuously deprived description of Da-sein, but it is antithetical to Merleau-Ponty's thematization of the sexed body and of carnal essences, as well as to his sustained engagements with artists such as Matisse and Rodin and with psychoanalysis. Beauty understood in terms of ideals of perfection (which are politicized in their resonance) can readily function as an instrument of propaganda, manipulation, and dominance. François Cheng, in his *Five Meditations on Beauty*—meditations initially carried out in a dialogical manner within a circle of artists, writers, psychoanalysts, and other intellectuals—finds that a specific form of evil stems from such perversion and abuse of beauty.[7]

Mindful, perhaps, not only of the challenges to and the marginalization or eclipse of beauty in twentieth-century art and art-theoretical discourse, as well as of beauty's sinister potential, Merleau-Ponty maintains an almost unbroken silence concerning beauty. Johnson lists a few instances in which the philosopher mentions it, showing that they function either as quotations from other writers or else in the context of his informal 1948 radio program *Causeries*.[8] It is worth noting, however, that, in his 1960–1961 course at the Collège de France, *L'ontologie cartésienne et l'ontologie d'aujourd'hui*, he offers a statement on beauty that is not only significant but relevant to the vision and practices of the artists discussed in this book.[9]

If Merleau-Ponty's near-silence concerning beauty may at times feel strained, his thought nonetheless offers a challenging conceptuality and vocabulary for rethinking and, perhaps, ultimately renaming it, so as to shed the burden of its rejection or trivialization. In "Eye and Mind," he cites Klee as to the painter's being "pierced through" (*transpercé*) by the universe, rather than expecting to pierce through any of its secrets.[10] If the metaphor of piercing suggests a certain violence that may be associated with the experience of beauty, Johnson's discussion of Rodin suggests rather its problematic kinship to ugliness. Johnson, seeking an understanding of beauty that (contrary to Barnett Newman's) would not contrast it with sublimity and demean it, but would rather cast it as sublimity's equal and as perhaps indissociable from it, points out that Rodin rejected the dichotomy between beauty as bodily perfection and the ugliness of its innumerable shortfalls. He recognized that art transfigures, but does not deny, the encompassing scope of the truth of reality.[11]

Beyond such respect for reality lies the problem of how to understand the transgressive coupling of abjection or repulsion with beauty, desire, and artistic validity. In "Beauty and Its Dilemmas," Olga M. Viso raises this question with regard to the painterly thematization of the human figure by Picasso, de Kooning, and Lucian Freud.[12] Drawing only on the artists discussed in this book, one could certainly add to her list much of the work of Kiki Smith, as well as some of the smeared, "debased," or "graffiti" works of Cy Twombly. Although this particular artistic preoccupation will not be in focus here, it does constitute an approach to problematizing beauty's ethical relevance.

One must agree with Arthur Danto's view that genuine artistic beauty must be "part of the meaning of the work, internally connected with its truth," in contrast to mere external attractiveness or "beautification."[13] He also reflects that beauty itself "might have yielded a significant means of criticizing the values of the society that they [the Dadaists who introduced beauty's debasement] deplored," but that in fact this debasement remained less than compelling as well as morally shallow.[14] Nonetheless, the integration of beauty with a work's meaning, truth, and power may not suffice to assure its strength in the sense of its uncompromising ethicality. Perhaps Riefenstahl's pursuit of beauty achieved such integration at least in part, while being nonetheless ethically questionable, to say the least. One needs to ask then by what strength beauty can, in its own right, resist becoming an instrument of exploitation, domination, or totalization.

I will here address this central question and its corollaries chiefly as they present themselves in the context of painting, which was, of course, Merleau-Ponty's own artistic focus (while beauty's debasement went hand in hand with declarations of painting's death). Painting has, thankfully, survived its premature, disdainful, and reiterated obituary;[15] but it is hoped that the questions raised here will, in future, be addressed, beyond painting, to the entire spectrum of visual art, as well as to arts that Merleau-Ponty neglected, notably the art of dance.

On Strong Beauty

So long as beauty functions chiefly or exclusively as a source of pleasure, it is not strong beauty. Rather than being something objectively or demonstratively given, strong beauty has the character of an *event*. What it manifests is not representational but revelatory. Its apparitional moment is characterized by an absence of transparency and by unforeseeability, which jointly frustrate any attempt at manipulation or control.[16]

For this reason, rather than just offering excitement or delight, it brings with it, in its presencing, an intensity akin to pain that may border on the scarcely bearable. It does so even in art that does not show anything intrinsically distressing, or that, like Agnes Martin's, is explicitly oriented toward transcendent perfection, joy, or happiness.[17] Nonetheless, what visual artworks that radiate strong beauty offer may be experienced, by those incapable of responding to their challenge, as just boringly "more bottles" depicted in still lifes by Morandi, or as being sketchy and awkward, such as Li Fangying's ink paintings of flowering plum.[18]

Nonetheless, and even though strong beauty in a work of art is independent of what, if anything, it may (re)present, certain (though not all) works that thematize horrific and distressing situations or events remain outside the pale of beauty, notwithstanding their artistic significance. One may think here of Goya's *Disasters of War* or of Picasso's iconic *Guernica*, to say nothing of photographic or cinematographic works that address the Shoah or recent terrorist events, such as the horrific one that has come to be known by an abbreviation of its (2001) date, 9/11. Contrary to Danto's claim, one did not have to wait for the Dada movement or for Duchamp to realize that significant art could be dissociated from beauty (without, for all that, being either infantilized or intellectualized).[19] To seek to appreciate works such as those mentioned in terms of beauty is not only to aestheticize horror and outrage, but it is also complicit with enlisting beauty for purposes of manipulation and domination. The complicity stems from beauty's being stripped, in these contexts, of any aspect of enigma or nontransparency.

Strong beauty's enigmatic character is linked to the fact that its apparitional moment is one of sheer encounter—an encounter that repudiates possession and that, as Henri Maldiney stresses, is oriented not solely toward the human Other but also toward the entire spectrum of living beings, and ultimately (beyond Maldiney) toward what Whitehead speaks of as the "ether of events" that pervades the cosmos.[20] Merleau-Ponty, meditating on this play of energies in relation to the key function of voids in the sculpture of Henry Moore, speaks of "a certain constitutive void . . . [that] supports the pretended positivity of things."[21] It is the empty yet dynamic insubstantiality or voidness of the dimension of manifestation that fundamentally gives strong beauty its strength.

In this context, it may be important to distinguish between *aisthēsis* in the double sense of sensory receptivity and feeling (approximated by the French term *sentir*) and perception, which, in the history of thought, tends to occlude the complexity of *aisthanesthai*. Merleau-Ponty's subtle interrogation of the "participations" that inform even basic sensory givens, or so-called sense data, and of the painter's "secret science" that interrogates them, aim to uncover a level of sheer donation, or of the upsurge of "wild being" prior to, and disruptive of, the perceptual quest for identification. The terminological assimilation of *aisthēsis* to perception somewhat obscures its anteriority to perceptual faith and to identification. *Aisthēsis*, unlike perception, involves a moment of sheer exposure and *pathos*; and this moment allows strong beauty to seize and grip one who experiences it, leaving her, in Merleau-Ponty's phrasing, "pierced through" by beauty's apparitional moment. In this sense, and in the words of Rilke's first *Duino Elegy* (cited by Johnson), "The beautiful is nothing / but the beginning of the terrible."[22]

Nature and Art

As Cheng felicitously expresses it, the universe appears in its beauty in the manner of a gift and not as a mere fact.[23] In his second lecture course on *Nature* of 1957–1958, Merleau-Ponty considers Portmann's researches on animal appearance as constituting neither a byproduct of biological processes nor as geared solely toward species survival (by offering information needed for optimal mate choice), but rather as the expression of the organism's distinctive life energy and creativity.[24] Aesthetic creativity is so prominent within nature that, among animals, it may issue in "unaddressed appearances" that are not offered to any possible eye.[25] In contrast to the Cartesian notion of a *creatio continua* that reduces nature to utter dependence, from moment to moment, on the divine creative act (thereby encouraging also the theistic argument from design), nature emerges, from these researches, as dynamically self-creating and as intrinsically striving for beauty.

One hesitates, nonetheless, to ascribe strong beauty to nature purely in itself, even when contemplating, say, majestic mountains traditionally held to be sacred, or the starscapes of the Southern sky. The reason is, to begin with, that the aesthetic appreciation of land- or starscapes involves no significant cognitive or moral component. In addition, strong beauty requires an encounter between the granting of nature and the human creative response. As Henri Maldiney puts it, "The irruption of being has meaning [*du sens*] only within the space of a human act."[26] Within the artwork itself any dualism between action and passion, together with subjectivity and objectivity, can be overcome, so that, as Merleau-Ponty writes, in painting it ultimately is "mute Being that comes of itself to manifest its own sense."[27]

In this context, it will be instructive to cast a quick glance at the arts of the garden. Gardens are, on the whole, suffused with a beauty that delights, enchants, supports contemplation, and optimally offers restoration or healing. Nonetheless, a search for strong beauty purely within the confines of the garden remains nearly fruitless, unless perhaps one turns to the almost counternatural art of dry Zen gardens such as Kyoto's iconic Ryōan-ji, created austerely out of rocks and raked sand, in a denial of nature's vegetal exuberance yet foregrounding the elemental interplay of sea and land.[28]

Strong beauty can characterize only an expressive work, that is to say, a work of art, at a greater remove from nature than most gardens. In the words of Jean-Louis Chrétien, its strength and power derive from the viewer's "being seized by the there-is," or being gripped by a donation that is fundamentally ontological.[29] In the moment of encounter, this donation may be experienced as transgressive and enigmatically transformative, exceeding one's preformed spectrum of possibilities. This power of strong beauty need nonetheless not be divorced, on the part of the artist, from an engagement with "content." For instance, the art of Felix Gonzalez-Torres (in media such as installation or photography) conjoins sociopolitical import concerning gay identity with both a poignant personal dimension of love, illness, and loss and with sheer aesthetic presence.

Strong Beauty in Art

It is noteworthy that, within the global art-historical spectrum, nonfigurative work possessed of strong beauty predates the modern era. Prominent examples include Chinese and Japanese calligraphy, such as, within the Chinese tradition, Huang T'ing-chien's (1451–1505) handscroll of biographies of Lien P'o and Ling Hsing-ju (undated), or within the Japanese tradition, the Zen-inspired Bokuseki (ink-trace) works of the Shingon Buddhist monk Jiun Onkō (1718–1804). In keeping with Merleau-Ponty's point that there is no basic dichotomy between figuration and abstraction, however, strong beauty also continues to characterize some contemporary figurative work (as has been seen with reference to Kiki Smith and Lucian Freud).

There is perhaps a certain sense today that, in keeping with Danto's reversal of Isaiah's "good tidings," art has for too long offered only "ashes for beauty." His point that a deliberate and sustained withholding of beauty may amount to a moral infraction rivaling that of the outrages that provoked its censure is challenging.[30] If some recent and contemporary artists have been motivated to create beauty anew (one may think here of Agnes Martin, Brice Marden, or Eva Hesse), they have mostly privileged nonfiguration, partly because it stays clear of the illusionism and the exclusionary and sexist politics that have long been associated with figuration, but also because artmaking, in its materiality, revealed its independence of representational references.

One may perhaps wonder, recalling Cézanne's well-known pronouncement that he owes his viewers "the truth in painting," and that he will deliver it,[31] whether an abandonment of figuration may prove detrimental to pictorial truth. Cézanne himself evidently did not consider pictorial truth to be univocal, given his highly differential explorations of key motifs, such as *Mont Sainte-Victoire*, the figure of his wife Hortense Fiquet, or his oneiric scenes of nude bathers in a landscape. His painterly truth is not one of adequation but is rather akin to Merleau-Ponty's own ontological interrogation, in that it seeks to recover a primordial and obliterated stratum of "wild being" on which humanity and culture have established themselves.[32] In a tribute to Cézanne, Maldiney writes that the painter has made of space "a fabric of events which are encounters, at once pictorial and cosmic."[33] Since his pictorial truth is devoid of univocity and positivity, it resists the dangers associated with figuration.

To sustain a focus on painting, it will be instructive to cast a brief glance at the nonfigurative art of Agnes Martin. In her extensive writings, she expresses a central, unquestioning devotion to beauty as "the mystery of life," and as indissociable from artistic validity, which in turn is linked for her to joy and to an intuitive rather than intellectually mediated (as in Platonism) contact with transcendent perfection.[34] Perfection remains for her insubstantial and beyond grasp, thus resisting hierarchization. The empty form, she writes (with reference to a pair of Chinese ceramics), "goes all the way to heaven"; and if one understands her praise of "Humility, the beautiful daughter," as a validation of her own work, one has to agree with her that "all her ways are empty."[35] In Tiffany Bell's assessment, this humility involved a collapsing of the distinction between painting and drawing, in that the paintings use "little paint, little color, and simple hand-drawn marks, which simultaneously map and veil the surface."[36]

When Martin took up painting again around 1974 in New Mexico after an extensive hiatus, having left New York's art world in 1967, she had also exchanged oil paint for acrylics and had given prominence to broad horizontal plane divisions in place of her earlier closely spaced linear grid, articulated by delicate pencil lines. The geometry of her horizontal or vertical bands was no longer necessarily marked by such lines nor enclosed within a demarcated frame. Barbara Haskell notes that, in these works, "lines and grids disappear into "subtly active fields of color," citing Rosalind Krauss's apt comment that they form "luminous containers for the shimmer of line."[37]

One owes to Krauss a perceptive analysis of Martin's work. Krauss, building on Kasha Linville's phenomenological study of how viewing distances alter the work's appearance, in a progression from a close-up foregrounding of materiality and facture to a middle distance effect of veiling, as though by mist, and finally, from far distance, to an impenetrable opacity,[38] understands these changes as effects within a painterly system that *must exclude* what is opposed to it, while nonetheless requiring and continually invoking it.[39] Drawing on Hubert Damisch's study on Brunelleschi's depiction of the Baptistry in Florence,[40] she reflects on perspective construction (which abidingly fascinated Merleau-Ponty) as a system of exclusions that mark the excluded (for Brunelleschi the changeable sky that, in his rendering of the Baptistry, is mirrored rather than depicted) *as unknowable and unrepresentable within the canons of the system*. The all-over grid, Krauss reflects, highlights these tensions by conjoining a quest for classical clarity and lucid definition, irrespective of vantage point, with a dissolution of the figure/ground articulation—a dissolution that is basically incompatible with classical clarity. It thus inscribes, within its systematicity, the excluded and unformed as a lack that nonetheless enables the system's self-articulation.[41]

An acknowledgment of the way that systems of form remain dependent on the excluded unformed is integral, and possibly essential, to strong beauty. Such a marking or acknowledgment contrasts with the sort of self-absolutization of a given system that Merleau-Ponty consistently rejects. Even though his insistence on the irrecusable primacy of the upsurge of the world or the lifeworld is in tension with an art that seeks, like Martin's, to turn its back on the world in a quest for pure transcendent perfection, an explicit acknowledgment of the lack symbolized by a differential marker that frustrates the "positivity" of a given system unites these perspectives in enabling strong beauty.

Krauss concludes by considering that the grid has tended, in recent art history, to merge more and more with its material support, giving rise to an "objectivist opticality." Thus, whereas Martin's effort to safeguard a classical ideal of perfection led her to define the grid structure in terms of a subtle acknowledgment of what it excluded, Ellsworth Kelly proceeded to materialize the grid.[42] This approach is exemplified for Krauss by Kelly's 1951 painting, *Colors for a Large Wall* (discussed in chapter 5), in which the color sequence of its sixty-four monochrome panels is left to chance. Unlike Martin (with whom, incidentally, he cultivated a warm art-centered friendship while they both lived at Coenties Slip in Manhattan during the late 1950s and early 1960s), Kelly rarely expresses an explicit concern for beauty. Quite apart from the issue of materializing the grid, however, the way that chance functions for him as an important interlocutor (notwithstanding his general practice of meticulous advance planning of his works) is important to his achievement of strong beauty.

Kelly began to integrate chance into his work during his formative years in France, drawing on his encounter with surrealism and on Jean Arp's practice of creating collages based on chance (a practice also taken up by Cy Twombly). Chance informed Kelly's work in two ways: first, by his articulating a vocabulary of forms found serendipitously within the natural and built environment; and second, by becoming integral to his creative process. Thus, for instance, *Spectrum Colors Arranged by Chance*[43] juxtaposes the geometry of the square grid, together with the optics of the spectrum, with color sequences left purely to chance, which is thus put into the position of the unpredictable excluded.

Kelly's engagement with chance is complemented by his attention to vegetal nature through his almost career-long practice of drawing plant forms from life. His dual integration of nature and chance with systematicity and meticulous planning served to distance his art from the formalist practices of Mondrian and Vantongerloo as well as Malevich, with whom some critics had associated it. It also functioned as an epistemological marker of the excluded unformed within, and indissociable from, the formal structure of a given visual system, counteracting the system's tendency to self-absolutization and enabling an achievement of strong beauty.

In "Eye and Mind," Merleau-Ponty reflects that, had Descartes examined "this other and more profound opening upon things given to us by the secondary qualities, notably color," he would have faced a universality without concept that might have motivated his intellectual heirs to treat Albertian perspective as "a special case of a vaster ontological power."[44] With a view to perspectival construction, and to the classical Florentine ideal of *disegno* as a whole, Merleau-Ponty tends to treat color as a constructivist system's essential excluded. Color, nonetheless, functions uneasily in this position since, within the legacy of seventeenth-century optics, it has itself been quantitatively analyzed and systematized. Newton's quantification of the color components of pure white light was greeted as aesthetically significant, in that it opened up the possibility of assimilating the harmonics of color to those of music, and ultimately even to the music of the spheres.[45]

Major tensions traverse what Merleau-Ponty calls "the dimension of color,"[46] including not only that between the energy fields of color on the one hand, and, on the other, color's quantitative analysis and systematization, but also between the chromas of the spectrum and those of the materiality of pigmentary color (which offers its own register of pictorial expression). How then does color enter into painting's alchemy of strong beauty?

One artist whose work addresses these issues is Gujarati-born Natvar Bhavsar who, as it happens, is also centrally concerned with beauty. Upon arriving in the United States in 1962, Bhavsar was drawn to the color-field tendencies within abstract expressionism, as well as to soak-and-stain color field painting, as practiced by Helen Frankenthaler and Morris Louis. Unlike Clement Greenberg, who critically championed color field painting, however, Bhavsar did not consider "opticality" to be incompatible with "tactility," or with painting's self-assertion of its own materiality. He sought instead a method of working with color that acknowledged both color's expression of the sheer luminous energy of the spectrum and its pigmentary materiality.

He developed a technique of sifting pure powdered pigments onto large-scale canvases soaked in a clear acrylic solution that functioned as a binder. Color is thus treated as a material substance in its own right, one whose rhythms and densities of application to the prone canvas (by means of screens, sieves, or funnels) configure the image as a record of the artist's bodily movement rather than as independent form. Bhavsar's chromatic environments are nonetheless sensitive to viewing distance, in a manner similar to Martin's work as discussed by Linville and Krauss. Up close, the viewer experiences the material granulation, densities, or dispersal of pigments. At a distance, however, one finds oneself immersed in luminous chromatic environments.[47] Bhavsar's art keeps in play the contrary tensions of color without any attempt at subjugation or exclusion. As he has acknowledged, he works *from within* color itself, rather than within systematic constraints and their concomitants of exclusion. Doing so, he is entranced by the beauty "of what just happens" (although such happenings are always subjected to his critical evaluation).[48] In his own view, the beauty attained does not contrast with or fall short of sublimity.[49] One may well question the need to retain sublimity as an aesthetic category (the more so since Kant, who gave it prominence, found it to be manifest chiefly in the experience of nature rather than of art, and specifically in the paling of art's, and beauty's, majesty and power before that of reason's recognition of moral law). Bhavsar's art has itself the event character of strong beauty and addresses the viewer within the space of what has been called "an oasis of contemplation."[50] In working directly out of color, his art achieves strong beauty not by acknowledging the essential excluded but rather by undercutting the very need for both systematicity and exclusion from the outset.

The Resilience of Strong Beauty

Strong beauty's foregrounding of its own event character is integral to its resilient resistance against being made an instrument of manipulation and domination. Its strength involves, somewhat paradoxically, a refusal to shrink from and cover over its own fragility, marked as it is by its invocation of the unfigurable excluded, or else by suspending the exclusionary structure of a visual system together with its systematicity. Chrétien (though commenting on Maldiney rather than on strong beauty) offers a felicitous formulation: "It is also a question of disengaging within ourselves this deep-seated fragility of exposure to the world, which is our only resource, covered over and obfuscated as it is by fears and prejudices of every sort—derisory fortifications that we set up against the ravaging (*la déchirure*) of existence."[51] For Merleau-Ponty, the sheer event character of strong beauty, realized in art, is more radically ontological. Kaushik, taking up Merleau-Ponty's reflection, in "Eye and Mind," that a painting is first of all *autofigurative*, so that, in breaking with representational thought, it becomes "a spectacle of nothing," argues that what he calls the autofigure marks being's intrinsic lack of self-sufficiency: it cannot "enact itself" without issuing into appearances and thus, as it were, into alienation.[52] Its fundamental moment is thus sheer genesis.[53] The artwork can directly and sensibly reveal this ontological movement of autofiguration, and in doing so it discloses, according to Kaushik, the multidimensional field structure of things in their coming to appearance.[54] It also discloses strong beauty in the tensional interrelation between delimitation and depth, or else in articulating itself out of a depth dimension anterior to delimitation.

When Merleau-Ponty writes, in "Eye and Mind," that "the painter's vision is a continual birth,"[55] he is not casting it as a matrix of innovative initiatory acts. Rather, in the context of his reflections on the reciprocity and reversibility (without coincidence) of seeing and being seen, and of action and passion becoming indiscernible, so that "one no longer knows who . . . paints and who is painted,"[56] birth is paradigmatically the immemorial event, anterior to subjectivity and passive, of taking birth, or being born. As Merleau-Ponty notes in his 1954–1955 lecture course on Institution and Passivity, "Birth [is not an act] of constitution, but institution of a future. Reciprocally, institution resides in the same *genre* of Being as birth, it is no more an act than it."[57] Birth reveals that we are always already situated in a field with multiple entry points and multiple thresholds between other and self.[58]

In coming to presence through a work of art, strong beauty does not offer exemplars that might be culturally or ideologically sanctioned. Since its very articulation of compelling form acknowledges what such form necessarily excludes, or else configures it in a manner anterior to form and to its exclusions, it must refuse absolutization and cannot be enlisted for purposes of manipulation. Its compelling fascination and power remain conjoined with an enigma of presencing that recalls Heidegger's notion of "the event of [the work's] createdness" (*das Ereignis seines Geschaffenseins*),[59] even though Heidegger's politics in the early to mid-1930s does not, in its relation to created works (which he does not limit to works of art) reflect this insight.

In visual art, strong beauty also comes into play at the precarious juncture between visual presencing and the invisibles that, in this presencing, it brings into play. Nothing is rendered invisible in this sense by being concealed or masked, whether within the often hauntingly enigmatic beauty of classical painting (such as certain works by Leonardo, Giorgione, or Vermeer), or within the contemporary works discussed. Rather, invisibles are in principle not another visible, rendered difficult of access, but rather, "the invisible is *there* without being object, it is pure transcendence, without an ontic mask. And the 'visibles' themselves, in the final analysis, are themselves also centered upon a nucleus of absence . . ."[60] Although the viewer remains free to look at classical or contemporary works without an explicit awareness of the invisibles indissociable from their visual articulation, the challenge to respond to this solicitation is offered unceasingly, and strong beauty is realized only in the ensuing response.

Merleau-Ponty also searchingly explores the interrelations of artistic creation with contingency and adversity. While his own focus, in this respect, is trained chiefly on Cézanne (in "Cézanne's Doubt"), the issue also concerns artists addressed in this book, perhaps predominantly Mitchell who (like her predecessors Monet and van Gogh) responded to adversity with an unquenchable passion to paint. In addressing the issue (without focusing on specific artists), Anna Caterina Dalmasso finds that the inextricable complicity of meaning or significance (*sens*) with contingency reveals "the inauthenticity of any absolute point of view."[61] In this elision of absolutizing, it thus shows itself to be complementary in its import to that of strong beauty.

In its engagement with the position of the essential excluded, or with depth structures that are anterior to both systematicity and exclusion, and in its relation to adversity and contingency, the realization of strong beauty in art is powerful in its own right, independent of whether or not works have sociopolitical "content." Even though at the time of this writing artists or curators may be called upon to "operate within the realm of cultural production [so as] to subvert the powerful and complex forces dominating this political moment,"[62] the artists discussed here have, with the possible or partial exception of Smith, tended toward an "absolute" rather than socioculturally engaged visual idiom. This study's intention has not, however, been to privilege this idiom; for as long as an artist's individual vision or style has the ability to bring one face to face with strong beauty, it remains challenging and powerful, whatever its allegiances; and strong beauty in any of its realizations does not tolerate the faint of heart.

Conclusion

More Ethereal Bodies

> Painting no longer weaves a presence: it is presence.
>
> —Octavio Paz, "Baudelaire as Art Critic"

Even though the choice of art and artists discussed in this book shows an acknowledged predilection for the nonfigurative or for figuration rethought and in question, as well as for artistic explorations of experience in its essentiality rather than its ordinary aspects (in keeping with Merleau-Ponty's rethinking of essences as "operative" in *The Visible and the Invisible*[1]), this predilection itself has been constantly questioned. It is questioned (together with art's relationship to beauty) in terms of both art's ethical import and of the unparalleled diversity of twentieth-century and contemporary art. Although, for these reasons, no artistic consensus has emerged nor could be expected, the emphasis has nevertheless been on a certain transmutation of material density into translucencies or into sheer energy and light, with light revealing not only visible reality but also the invisibles inseparable from visual presencing. Thus, for instance, Morandi's art drains ordinary still life objects of their meaning and formal integrity, leaving sometimes only their memory distilled into light, while Mitchell recreates the experience of landscape and place in terms of light's declensions into color and of gestural marks in space. While Twombly's late *Bacchus* and *Camino Real* cycles work with sheer transgressive energy rather than material form, the *Gaeta Set (for the Love of Fire and Water)* of 1981 " 'translates,' " as Jacobus puts it, "light's writing on water—refracted, obscured, stilled . . . ," and leaving ultimately only a translucent green shimmer.[2]

Kelly's long-standing painterly preoccupation with the spectrum achieves independence from materiality only through the use of stained glass in his posthumously completed architectural (and artistically all-inclusive) work *Austin*. It will be helpful briefly to revisit these artistic practices, at least to the very selective extent that they are discussed in or relevant to this book, and to reflect on their import.

Transmuting Materiality into Light

Although Morandi was certainly a master of classical still life painting, his quest was increasingly not for mimesis but for the mutable configurations of forms, as well as their erosion and disfiguration, by light. Rather than having any stable identity or suggesting what Heidegger calls the infrangible self-containment of things, forms may merge with or ambiguously displace one another, or be indicated only by marks suggestive of their absence. This dematerialization of things by light and the spatial disorientation it makes for are perhaps not as unique to "modern" painting (in its contrast with "classical thought") as Merleau-Ponty thinks. For instance, El Greco (familiar with the heritage of Michelangelo, Titian, and other masters of the Florentine, Roman, and Venetian Renaissance schools) removed figures and figural scenes from the contexts of narrative time, place, and action, setting them instead within dramas of light, which may be both meteorological and transcendent. The draperies of his figures, dramatically modeled by light, often echo the drama of light in his turbulent skies. However, given the system of ecclesiastical or aristocratic patronage, figures and scenes had to remain recognizable and conform to biblical, devotional, or theological orthodoxy, or else to secular conventions, whereas Morandi was free to explore vision as such and as articulated in response to light.

Although Smith's installations do not contest materiality, they deliteralize it and play with light's aspects of mystery and transcendence. In this respect, her motif of inspiration (often symbolized by a bird's descent) may recall at times El Greco's descending dove (symbol of the Holy Spirit) in radiant light. Since she is expert at working with glass, she can explore transparence, translucency, iridescence, and veilings, as well as the luminosity of colored glass. She also foregrounds the achromatic colors, black and white, which, respectively, absorb or reflect the entirety of the spectrum, so that no hues become apparent. Mitchell, for her part, does not accept the facile assimilation of brightness (particularly as achieved through the painter's use of white) to light, nor does she accept that light becomes apparent through its revelation of defined figures or forms. What it reveals for her through color and gestural form in space are ultimately dimensions of feeling mediated by memory and elusive to verbal expression.

For Kelly, light is primordially expressed through its refraction into the seven colors of the spectrum visible to normal human sight (many insects and birds can see in the ultraviolet range, and snakes can see infrared). Kelly's architectural use of stained glass disencumbers his engagement with the hues of the spectrum of the materiality of paint as well as of the fixity of supports. Light is free to move as it will, reconfiguring architectural spaces. Artistic explorations of the dematerializing power of light converge with the philosophical exploration of the ungroundedness of manifestation and of its radically differential character. The ways in which some recent and contemporary art has explored the powers of light thus render it even more challenging to classical philosophical conceptions of vision and the image than Merleau-Ponty recognized.

Traces at the Verge

In Twombly's explorations of writing's wordless essence through quasi-inscription menaced by effacements, or in his defacements, superpositions, and veilings, identity remains elusive. It is, however, not simply absent but hovers hauntingly at the verge, perpetually promised yet inexorably withheld. The interlaced bodies of image and text are unstable, veering readily from one nearly antithetical conventionally recognized position to another, such as from lyricism to brutality, from the license of artistic creativity and eroticism to the trauma of war, or from beauty to degradation; and where names are legibly inscribed, they often function as markers of irreparable loss. What Twombly's art focuses on is not identities but the unforeseeable and sheer event character of manifestation; and therefore it is capable of crossing out customary antithetical notions, such as the familiar mutually exclusive binaries of classical philosophical discourse (reality and appearance may serve as a key example). Mutability is also essential to the Mediterranean, and particularly the Greek, imagination that Twombly continually explored: deities are shape-shifters and their gifts to lesser divinities (such as nymphs) or mortals, or the curses they may inflict, often involve changing form: Thus, Daphne the nymph becomes a plant, as does Minthe, but in her case through a curse due to divine jealousy. Ontological or natural categories are unstable and identities transient and negotiable; and in this context, binaries have no place. Binaries are also crossed out in Smith's art, but on a level of more concrete, if problematized, identifications, such as those of gender or of the position of humanity in relation to animality and to cosmic and historical emplacement.

It is significant that Twombly privileges the elements of both water and fire that are antithetical yet united in their extreme mutability (one does not perhaps give enough recognition to the astonishing mutability of water that can take the forms of liquid, solid, or gas, to say nothing of its continual interactions with light). To reconsider mutability once more, it is philosophically articulated, before its eventual rejection by Platonism, in Heraclitus's and Empedocles's delineation of cosmic cycles conjoining antitheticals or else the phases of unity and fragmentation.

At the verge, in any case, the trace remains powerfully active and enters into its own domain, which is the freedom (but not the randomness) of institution, as Merleau-Ponty thematizes it. Institution operates, of course, on multiple levels, including those of the psyche and of art as well as of the public and political domain. It enables one to recognize the central importance of the long marginalized aesthetic and artistic dimensions to political praxis and ethicality.

Transparencies of Line

Mimetic fidelity may be not only unnecessary but sometimes even a hindrance to artistically conveying the vital essence of forms of life that have long been demoted either to insignificance or to mere decorative motifs, along with being philosophically disregarded. Such is, of course, the status of vegetal life that Merleau-Ponty ignores in the context of thinking through the implications of the "new biology" of the mid-twentieth century for the philosophical understanding of animality. Although it is true that contemporary art focused on plant life has, on the whole, tended toward essentialization and abstraction (even where it may employ the resources of hyperrealism, as in some of McEwen's work),[3] it still faces the challenge of breaking with the established conventions that underlie the modalities of seeing that make for Merleau-Pontyan "profane vision."

Kelly's practice of plant drawing and lithography has surpassed these conventions by interpreting plant forms as pure linear and rhythmic configurations within pictorial space. It encourages a way of seeing that gives vegetal forms a certain translucency that desubstantializes them, while also emphasizing their mutability and transience. Identification is thus persistently called into question. Kelly has, for instance, sequentially and side by side drawn different views of the inflorescence of a calla lily by slowly rotating the plant held in his free hand. Unlike images that facilitate identification based on established iconic schemata, none of Kelly's drawn aspects of a single plant form are privileged or iconic, and their conjunction calls for new modalities of visual encounter. At the same time, Kelly's drawings offer a fresh way to experience the autonomous dance of line in space that Merleau-Ponty thematizes and celebrates in "Eye and Mind," chiefly with reference to Klee's reflections on freeing line from the prosaic tasks of depiction. Kelly's lines, however, are not pure abstract linear rhythms but remain persistently those of contour drawing. There are, of course, no contours or outlines given in nature, while nonetheless contours are descriptive. Kelly's drawings call attention to both aspects of this near-paradox by conjoining the free, inventive spontaneity of line with the persistent (and well-informed) evocation of vegetal forms. They thus situate the viewer in a persistent tension between invention and description, and once again at the verge.

Prospect

Faced with the trivialization of images, which are ubiquitous in contemporary culture and seem to become ever more meaningless the more they are graphically inventive, colorful, and sometimes strident, art may resort to desubstantialization in quest of a more meditative as well as challenging approach to the image, although this is not its only option. One thinks, for instance, of works that bypass the image by compelling direct immersive encounter, such as Walter de Maria's *Lightning Field* in Quemado, New Mexico. To stay, however, within the framework of this discussion, it is worth considering the notion of "slow painting" as understood by Stephen Westfall (in his view it encompasses both figuration and abstraction), but the notion would here need to be broadened to address, beyond painting, a wider spectrum of visual art.[4] The "slowness" involved does not exclude gestural or even action painting, but it allows the artist to disappear into his or her work, cultivating a certain anonymity (in keeping with Merleau-Ponty's emphasis on anonymity and generality) instead of foregrounding his or her subjectivity. The viewer likewise is challenged to immerse herself in the painting or other artwork, which can genuinely, yet changeably, reveal itself only in response to the time or times of contemplation and refuses to be objectified.

Certainly, such slow painting can be found across the contemporary spectrum, including perhaps Jasper Johns's late introspective and enigmatic works, as almost always in the medium of encaustic. Westfall characterizes slow painting as embedding "a premonition of something potentially enormous [and] held in reserve that can only be revealed slowly."[5] Westfall calls particular (but not exclusive) attention to the work of Susan Frecon and Jessica Dickinson. Frecon asserts that hers are "paintings that you experience, there is no story,"[6] while Dickinson's scarred yet intensive monochromes incorporate the accidents of time. The work of these painters (who, in their explorations of what may count as more ethereal bodies, nonetheless engage intensively with the dense materiality of their media) signals the need for art and art-critical discourse to respond to the phenomenological analysis that Merleau-Ponty initiated and that he focused insistently on painting, while also attending to the wider spectrum of visual art in quest of what Carbone terms not simply vision, but *voyance*. Both art itself and its philosophical exploration remain in need of carrying forward this Merleau-Pontyan initiative.

Notes

In citing works in the notes, short titles generally follow full citations. Works frequently cited have been identified by the following abbreviations:

EM Maurice Merleau-Ponty. "Eye and Mind." Translated by Michael B. Smith. In *The Merleau-Ponty Reader*, edited by Leonard Lawlor and Ted Toadvine. Evanston: Northwestern University Press, 2007.

N Maurice Merleau-Ponty. *La nature. Notes du cours du Collège de France*. Paris: Seuil, 1995. English translation by Robert Vallier, edited by Dominique Séglard, *Nature: Course Notes from the Collège de France*. Evanston: Northwestern University Press, 2003.

OE Maurice Merleau-Ponty. *L'œil et l'esprit*. Paris: Gallimard, 1964.

PhP Maurice Merleau-Ponty. *Phenomenology of Perception*. Translated by Donald A. Landes. London: Routledge, 2012.

TP Efrem Tavoni. *Morandi, Disegni, Catalogo Generale*. Milan: Electa, 1964.

V Lamberto Vitali. *Morandi, Catalogo Generale*, 2 vols. Milan: Electa, 1977.

VI Maurice Merleau-Ponty. *Le visible et l'invisible, suivi de notes de travail*. Paris: Gallimard, 1964. English translation by Alphonso Lingis, *The Visible and the Invisible*. Evanston: Northwestern University Press, 1968.

Introduction

1. Galen A. Johnson, *The Retrieval of the Beautiful: Thinking Through Merleau-Ponty's Aesthetics* (Evanston: Northwestern University Press, 2010).

2. Rajiv Kaushik, *Art, Language, and Figure in Merleau-Ponty: Excursions in Hyper-Dialectic* (London: Bloomsbury, 2013). At the time of this writing, Kaushik's

new book, *Merleau-Ponty between Philosophy and Symbolism: The Matrixed Ontology*, is soon to appear from State University of New York Press.

3. Mauro Carbone, *The Flesh of Images: Merleau-Ponty between Painting and Cinema*, trans. Marta Nijhuis (Albany: State University of New York Press, 2015). See also his *Sullo schermo dell'estetico: la pittura, il cinema e la filosofia da fare* (Milan: Mimesis, 2008). For a full account of his relevant writings, see the bibliography of Anna Caterina Dalmasso, *Le corps, c'est l'écran: la philosophie du visuel de Merleau-Ponty* (Paris: Éditions Mimésis, 2018).

4. See note 3, above.

5. Maurice Merleau-Ponty, *Le monde sensible et le monde de l'expression*, texte annoté et établi par Emmanuel de Saint Aubert et Stefan Kristensen (Geneva: Metis, 2011).

6. Unfortunately, this work so far remains unpublished.

7. David Morris, *Merleau-Ponty's Developmental Ontology* (Evanston: Northwestern University Press, 2018).

8. Morris, *Merleau-Ponty's Developmental Ontology*, 202.

9. Maurice Merleau-Ponty, *L'œil et l'esprit* (Paris: Gallimard, 1964), 76, 87. English translation by Michael B. Smith, "Eye and Mind," in *The Merleau-Ponty Reader*, ed. Leonard Lawlor and Ted Toadvine (Evanston: Northwestern University Press, 2007), 372, 375. These texts will be referred to, respectively, as OE and EM. I have habitually modified rather than straightforwardly cited translations of Merleau-Pontian texts.

10. Carbone, *The Flesh of Images*, 1–6.

11. Understanding "vision" here in the sense in which an artist can be said to realize his or her vision.

12. This injunction originates with Max Beckmann.

13. See Martin Heidegger, "Der Ursprung des Kunstwerkes," in *Holzwege*, 4th ed. (Frankfurt: Klostermann, 1963), 7–68.

14. *Verlässlichkeit* is cognate to the verb *verlassen* (to abandon), which, in its reflexive form (*sich verlassen auf*) comes to mean to rely on or put one's trust in.

15. Martin Heidegger, "Das Ding," in *Vorträge und Aufsätze*, vol. 2, 3rd ed. (Pfullingen: Neske, 1967), 37–65.

16. OE, 14; EM, 353.

17. Maurice Merleau-Ponty, "Indirect Language and the Voices of Silence," trans. Michael B. Smith, in *The Merleau-Ponty Aesthetics Reader*, ed. Galen A. Johnson (Evanston: Northwestern University Press, 1993), 117.

18. Interestingly, Stefan Kristensen, in "Flesh and the Machine: Toward a Transversal Ontology with Merleau-Ponty and Guattari," *Chiasmi* 18 (2006): 180, n. 29, quotes Deleuze and Guattari, in *A Thousand Plateaus*, to argue that "painters . . . may be much more open socially, much more political, and less controlled from without or within. That is because each time they paint, they must create a

phylum, and they must do so on the basis of bodies of light which they themselves produce . . ."

19. Maurice Merleau-Ponty, *La Nature. Notes de cours du Collège de France* (Paris: Seuil, 1995), 188. English translation by Robert Vallier, edited by Dominique Séglard, *Nature: Course Notes from the Collège de France* (Evanston: Northwestern University Press, 2003), 190. This volume will be referred to as N.

20. Richard O. Prum, *The Evolution of Beauty: How Darwin's Forgotten Theory of Mate Choice Shapes the Animal World—and Us* (New York: Doubleday, 2017). Prum's book was published when the writing of this book was already essentially complete, so that it could not be referenced as fully as I would have desired. As to Portmann, see his *Die Tiergestalt: Studien über die Bedeutung der tierischen Erscheinung*, 2nd rev. ed. (Basel: Friedrich Reinhardt, 1960).

21. Portmann put forward his theory of unaddressed appearances only in the second (1960) edition of his *Die Tiergestalt*. Merleau-Ponty's discussion of Portmann's work in his second Nature course (1957–1958) does not address it.

22. Prum, *The Evolution of Beauty*, 558.

Chapter 1

1. I quote the remark as conveyed by Maria Cristina Bandera in "Contemporanità di Morandi / Morandi Our Contemporary," in *Giorgio Morandi*, ed. Maria Cristina Bandera and Marco Franciolli (Milan: Silvana Editoriale, 2012), 19.

2. See Tricia Y. Paik, *Ellsworth Kelly*, with contributions from Gavin Delahunty, Gary Garrels, Richard Schiff, and Robert Storr (London: Phaidon, 2015), 32.

3. OE, 76; EM, 87.

4. As quoted by Bandera from Paul Auster, *Sunset Park* (New York: 1910), in "Morandi Our Contemporary," 15–17.

5. Giorgio Morandi in a radio interview of 1955, as quoted by Bandera, "Morandi Our Contemporary," 19.

6. Carbone, *The Flesh of Images*, 59.

7. Janet Abramovicz, *Giorgio Morandi: The Art of Silence* (New Haven: Yale University Press, 2004). See also Siri Hustvedt, "The Drama of Perception: Looking at Morandi," in *Giorgio Morandi*, ed. Maria Cristina Bandera and Marco Franciolli (Milan: Silvana Editoriale, 2012), 267.

8. *Pittura metafisica* (a key exponent of which was Giorgio de Chirico) was closely associated and contemporaneous with the publication of the avant-garde journal *Valori Plastici* (Plastic Values) between 1918 and 1922.

9. Siri Hustvedt, *Mysteries of the Rectangle: Essays on Painting* (Hudson: Princeton Architectural Press, 2006).

10. Heidegger, "Der Ursprung des Kunstwerkes," 7–65. My translations.

11. Heidegger, "Das Ding," 37–55. Translations are mine.
12. Heidegger, "Das Ding," 55. I am, of course, here disregarding the tradition of Western thought that disregards so-called nonsentient nature, affirming with Spinoza (and arguably seconded by Leibniz) that *omnia animata sunt* (All things are animate).
13. This is a sense of the phenomenological dictum "zu den Dingen selbst." Usually translated as "to the things themselves," it is better understood as "back to what is at issue" or "to what concerns us."
14. Heidegger, "Das Ding," 53.
15. Heidegger, "Das Ding," 51.
16. Jacques Taminiaux, "The Origin of 'The Origin of the Work of Art,'" in *Poetics, Speculation, and Judgment: The Shadow of the Work of Art from Kant to Phenomenology*, ed. and trans. Michael Gendre (Albany: State University of New York Press, 1993). The three versions of "The Origin of the Work of Art" are Heidegger's lecture of November 13, 1935, followed closely by the "first elaboration," and in the fall of 1936 by the text included in *Holzwege*. See Taminiaux's essay for bibliographical details.
17. Taminiaux, "The Origin of 'The Origin of the Work of Art,'" 167. Heidegger's understanding of art in the context of *technē*, and his rejection, traced by Taminiaux in the writings of 1933–1935, of the everyday and commonplace, have political import. Although this issue is not thematic in this book, some discussion of it can be found in chapter 3.
18. Merleau-Ponty, *Le visible et l'invisible, suivi de notes de travail*, 71; English translation by Lingis, *The Visible and the Invisible*, 220. Hereafter, cited by the abbreviation VI.
19. "Transcendence of the Thing and Transcendence of the Phantasm," May 1959, VI 245; 191.
20. VI, 214; 167.
21. OE, 76; EM 372.
22. Interview with Edouard Roditi, 1958, as quoted by Bandera, "Morandi Our Contemporary," 29.
23. See VI, chap. 4, "Le chiasme" (The chiasm).
24. VI, 174; 132–133.
25. See VI, 177; 134.
26. VI, 178; 135.
27. Hustvedt, "The Drama of Perception: Looking at Morandi," 265.
28. *Natura morta con drapo giallo* (Still life with yellow cloth). Oil on canvas, 68 × 70 cm. V, 101 (Florence: Fondazione di Studi di Storia Dell' Arte Roberto Longhi). The V refers to Lamberto Vitali, *Morandi, Catalogo Generale*, 2 vols. (Milan: Electa, 1977), and the expanded second edition of 1983. Commentators include Siri Hustvedt and Simona Tosini Pizzetti.

29. OE, 87; EM, 376.
30. See VI, 174 and 132–133; and OE, 24; EM, 346.
31. VI, 179; 152.
32. VI, 198; 151.
33. *Natura morta* (Still life), 1936, TP, 1936 / 2. Black pencil on paper, 25 × 31 cm., private collection. TP refers to Efrem Tavoni, *Morandi, Disegni, Catalogo Generale* (Milan: Electa, 1964).
34. Simona Tosini Pizzetti, in Bandera, "Morandi Our Contemporary," 72.
35. OE, 64; EM, 369.
36. Hustvedt, "The Drama of Perception," 257.
37. Maurice Merleau-Ponty, "Cézanne's Doubt," in *Sense and Non-Sense*, trans. Hubert L. Dreyfus and Patricia Allen Dreyfus (Evanston: Northwestern University Press, 1991), 14, 16.
38. *Landscape*, 1961.Oil on canvas, 16 × 14 in. (35 × 30 cm.). Collection of Ida Marmotti Lombardini. V, 1252.
39. Abramovicz, *Giorgio Morandi*, 228.
40. See, for instance, *Landscape*, 1963. Oil on canvas, 10 × 20 in. (25 × 50 cm.). Formerly Plaza Collection. V. 1334.
41. Maurice Merleau-Ponty, "L'homme et l'adversité," in *Signes* (Paris: Gallimard, 1960), 366. English translation by Richard C. McCleary, "Man and Adversity," in *Signs* (Evanston: Northwestern University Press, 1964).
42. See Abramovicz, *Giorgio Morandi*, chap. 2.
43. Merleau-Ponty, "L'homme et l'adversité," 304.
44. See Abramovicz, *Giorgio Morandi*, 93.
45. The name stood for both a rural and environmentally sustainable utopia situated "somewhere between Siena and Florence," and a loose association of antibourgeois rebellious spirits. See Abramovicz, *Giorgio Morandi*, 118.
46. Abramovicz, *Giorgio Morandi*, 118.
47. Abramovicz, *Giorgio Morandi*, 117.
48. Abramovicz, *Giorgio Morandi*, 136.
49. Abramovicz, *Giorgio Morandi*, 135.
50. *Natura morta* (Still life), 1936. Oil on canvas, 50 × 60 cm. Private collection. V, 207.
51. Abramovicz, *Giorgio Morandi*, 145.
52. Abramovicz, *Giorgio Morandi*, 116. Arcangeli (who had been Morandi's favorite student) is the author of *Giorgio Morandi* (Milan: Einaudi, 1964). Unfortunately, Arcangeli's unwillingness to conform to the Morandi "myth" led to a break in their close friendship.
53. Abramovicz, *Giorgio Morandi*, 168.
54. *Natura morta*, 1942. Oil on canvas, 47.5 × 40.5 cm. Parma, Fondazione de Magnani Rocca. V, 384.

55. See Bandera and Franciolli, *Giorgio Morandi*, 96.
56. As quoted by Pizzetti from Arcangeli's monograph, *Giorgio Morandi*, in Bandera and Franciolli, *Giorgio Morandi*, 96.
57. Maurice Merleau-Ponty, "New Working Notes from the Period of *The Visible and the Invisible*," Note of 13 May 1960, in *The Merleau-Ponty Reader*, ed. Leonard Lawlor and Ted Toadvine (Evanston: Northwestern University Press, 2007), 440. I have slightly altered the translation.
58. Abramovicz, *Giorgio Morandi*, 222.
59. *Natura morta*, 1959.Watercolor on paper, 16.2 × 20.7 cm. Bern, Oberholzer Collection. TP, 1959–1939.
60. See Pisini's comments on this watercolor and a related oil painting in Bandera and Franciolli, *Giorgio Morandi*, 192.
61. Merleau-Ponty, "Cézanne's Doubt," 14.
62. See Heidegger, "Das Ding," 39–41 and 46–50.
63. Merleau-Ponty, Working Note of May 1959, VI, 245; 191.
64. OE, 81; EM, 374.
65. OE, 63; EM, 368.

Chapter 2

1. *Ineinander* (literally, "into one another," which might perhaps be translated as "inter-being") is one of the Husserlian terms that Merleau-Ponty likes to borrow. See Bernhard Waldenfels's comments on the term in "Going and Coming of Time," in *Time, Memory, Institution: Merleau-Ponty's New Ontology of Self*, ed. David Morris and Kym McLaren (Athens: Ohio University Press, 2015), 216–237.
2. See her comments to Christopher Lyon in an interview titled "Free Fall: Kiki Smith on Her Art," Helaine Posner, *Kiki Smith* (Boston: Bullfinch, 1998), 37–43.
3. See N, 208.
4. Lyon, "Free Fall," 39.
5. Lyon, "Free Fall," 39.
6. The second Nature course of 1957–1958, focused on *Animality, the Human Body, and the Passage to Culture*, is extant in the form of an anonymous auditor's lecture notes. Quotations therefore may not reproduce Merleau-Ponty's own phrasing or thought. For the quotation, see N, 187. See Portmann, *Die Tiergestalt*. Given his death in early 1961, Merleau-Ponty was unable to consult this revised edition, which, importantly, recognized "unaddressed appearances," that is, a visual creativity not addressed to any possible eye. For discussion, see my *Tracing Expression in Merleau-Ponty: Aesthetics, Philosophy of Biology, and Ontology* (Evanston: Northwestern University Press, 2013), chap. 5.
7. N, 187.

8. "Lynne Tillman in Conversation with Kiki Smith, New York, Sept. 9, 2004," in *Kiki Smith: A Gathering, 1980–2005*, ed. Siri Engberg (Minneapolis: Walker Art Center, 2006), 38–41. Smith also frequently speaks of embracing and putting to affirmative use what is used against one, such as, for women, their assimilation to nature.

9. Maurice Merleau-Ponty, *The Prose of the World*, ed. Claude Lefort, trans. John O'Neill (Evanston: Northwestern University Press, 1991), 83. Merleau-Ponty himself left this book manuscript unfinished, ceasing work on it in the fall or winter of 1951–1952. This text will be referred to as PW.

10. For extensive pictorial documentation and discussion (from a Jungian perspective), see Buffie Johnson, *Lady of the Beasts: Ancient Images of the Goddess and Her Sacred Animals* (San Francisco: Harper & Row, 1988). The central issue is the way in which perception is from the outset informed by culture, as to which see Anna Caterina Dalmasso's discussion in *Le corps c'est l'écran*, 185.

11. *Rapture*, 2001. Bronze, 67.25 × 62 × 26.25 in. (170.8 × 157.5 × 66.7 cm.). Collection of the artist. Smith has identified the figure as Sainte Geneviève, discussed later in this chapter.

12. *Born*, 2002. Bronze, 39 × 101 × 24 in. (99.1 × 256.5 × 61 cm.). Collection of the artist.

13. *Carrier (Standing Woman Carrying Wolf)*, 2004. Collage and ink on Nepalese paper and methyl cellulose, 91 × 56 in. (231.1 × 142.2 cm.) and 76 × 56 in. (193 × 42.2 cm.). Collection of the artist.

14. *Tied to Her Nature*, 2002. Bronze, 12.5 × 21 × 7.75 in. (31.8 × 53.3 × 19.7 cm.). Whitney Museum of American Art.

15. Lyon, "Free Fall," 39.

16. *Wolf Girl*, 1999. From the series *Blue Prints*. Etching, aquatint, and drypoint on molded paper, 20 × 16 in. (50.8 × 40.6 cm.). Published by Thirteen Moons, New York.

17. *Daughter* (in collaboration with Margaret de Wys), 1999. Nepalese paper, bubble wrap, methyl cellulose, hair, fabric, glass, and motion-activated soundtrack. The Ann and Mell Schaffer family collection.

18. See Marina Warner, "Wolf-Girl, Soul-Bird: The Mortal Art of Kiki Smith," in *Kiki Smith: A Gathering, 1980–2005*, ed. Siri Engberg (Minneapolis: Walker Arts Center, 2006), 52.

19. Lyon, "Free Fall," 39.

20. Posner, *Kiki Smith*, 32.

21. Lyon, "Free Fall," 38–39.

22. Lyon, "Free Fall," 40.

23. *Black Bird*, 1996. Feathers, muslin, polyester fiberfill, silver, gold, thread, wood, wire, and enamel paint, 17 × 13 × 16 in. (43.2 × 33 × 40.3 cm.). Collection Susan and Lewis Manilow, Chicago.

24. *Head with Bird*, 1994. Phosphorous bronze and white bronze; unique edition, 14.125 × 12 × 6.25 in. (35.9 × 30.5 × 15.9 cm.). Collection of Vicky and Kent Logan.

25. *Crows* (*Six Crows*), 1995. Six units. Silicon bronze, sizes and installation dimensions variable. Collection of Lenore and Richard Niles, San Francisco. *Jersey Crows*, 1995. Silicon bronze. Twenty-seven units, each 6.25 × 17 × 11 in. to 16 × 19 × 23.5 in. Installation dimensions variable. Private collection. The distressing incident of the crows' poisoning is far from unique; quite recently far larger numbers of migrating geese were killed as they landed in a body of water industrially polluted with acid.

26. OE, 21; EM, 355.

27. Helaine Posner and Marina Warner offer similar quotations from personal exchanges with Smith. See Posner, *Kiki Smith*, 22; and Warner, "Wolf-Girl, Soul-Bird," 41, 46.

28. Maurice Merleau-Ponty, "Faith and Good Faith," in *Sense and Non-Sense*, trans. Hubert L. Dreyfus and Patricia Allen Dreyfus (Evanston: Northwestern University Press, 1991), 172–181; and Maurice Merleau-Ponty, "In Praise of Philosophy," in *In Praise of Philosophy and Other Essays*, ed. John Wild and James Edie, trans. John O'Neill (Evanston: Northwestern University Press, 1988), 3–47. Carbone traces in Gauguin's art (after the painter's move to Tahiti) the deconstruction of Christian flesh (*The Flesh of Images*, 25), but then Merleau-Ponty's engagement with Christian flesh (and, for that matter, Smith's) does not straightforwardly address Christian flesh.

29. Merleau-Ponty, "Faith and Good Faith," 175.

30. Merleau-Ponty, "In Praise of Philosophy," 30–31.

31. Merleau-Ponty, "In Praise of Philosophy," 31.

32. The original source of this variously quoted narrative is David Frankel, "In Her Own Words," in Helaine Posner, *Kiki Smith* (Boston: Bullfinch Press, 1998), 41.

33. One may note that peacocks are not necessarily birds of brilliant color; I have seen hauntingly beautiful white peacocks in Indonesia.

34. Portmann, *Die Tiergestalt*.

35. *Pietà*, 1999. Lithograph on Nepalese paper and methyl cellulose, 92 × 132 ½ in. (233.7 × 334 cm.). Collection of the Museum of Modern Art, New York.

36. *Tale*, 1992. Wax, pigment, and papier-mâché, 160 × 23 × 23 in. Collection of Jeffrey Deitsch. Among the work's severest critics when it was first shown as part of the 1999 exhibition *Sensation* at the Brooklyn Museum was Philippe de Montebello, the former director of New York's Metropolitan Museum.

37. Posner, *Kiki Smith*, 21.

38. See Lyon, "Free Fall," 39.

39. Maurice Merleau-Ponty, *Phenomenology of Perception*, trans. Donald A. Landes (London: Routledge, 2012), 136. This work will be referred to as PhP.

40. Warner, "Wolf-Girl, Soul-Bird," 47.

41. Warner appreciates and elaborates on art's character of play but does not see it as the antidote to petrification. "Quickening," of course, is a term used to refer to a pregnant woman's first feeling the movements of her fetus, and it shows the recognition of movement's attesting to life.

42. OE, 62–63; EM, 368–369.

43. "Lynne Tillman in Conversation with Kiki Smith," 40. This is also the locus of Smith's comment as to playing with meaning.

44. N, 188.

45. Johnson, *The Retrieval of the Beautiful*, 228. It was the critic Harold Rosenberg who initially foregrounded the event character of mid-twentieth-century American painting. See Sebastian Smee, *The Art of Rivalry: Four Friendships, Betrayals, and Breakthroughs in Modern Art* (New York: Random House, 2017), 335–339.

46. "Lynn Tillman in Conversation with Kiki Smith," 39.

47. Kiki Smith, *Sojourn*, Brooklyn Museum, 2010, was the fourth site-specific installation Smith created in the wider context of a unitary project. It was preceded by related installations at Museum Haus Esters, Krefeld, Germany, 2008, which traveled on to Kunsthalle Nürnberg, and to the Fundació Juan Miró, Barcelona, in 2009. One site feature that made the Brooklyn Museum's show haunting was the placement of figures in the museum's period rooms adjacent to the gallery.

48. Kiki Smith, *Virgin Mary*, 1992. Beeswax, microcrystalline wax, cheesecloth, wood, and pigment, 26 × 36 × 24 in. Collection of Emily Fisher Landau, New York. Commenting on this work, Linda Nochlin describes the figure of the Virgin as resembling "an anatomical écorchée . . . close to the condition of meat and tendon, a torture victim rather than a succorer." See her "Unholy Postures," in *Kiki Smith: A Gathering, 1980–2005*, 35. Smith, however, effaces the antithesis between torture victim and succorer, which once again bespeaks a profound engagement with her Catholic heritage.

49. "Lynn Tillman in Conversation with Kiki Smith," 40.

50. Heidegger, "Nachwort" (Postscript) to "Der Ursprung des Kunstwerkes," 67. My translation.

51. As discussed in chapter 1, Heidegger gives greater recognition to things of use in the 1950 essay "The Thing." It remains questionable, however, whether this recognition approaches an affirmation of everyday life.

52. Catherine J. Morris, *Kiki Smith, Sojourn*, press release, February 2010.

53. Siri Hustvedt, "Vermeer's Annunciation," in *Mysteries of the Rectangle: Essays on Painting* (Hudson: Princeton Architectural Press, 2006), 11–16.

54. Yasmil Raymond Ventura, with Max Andrews, "Chronology," in *Kiki Smith: A Gathering, 1980–2005*, ed. Siri Engberg (Minneapolis: Walker Arts Center, 2006), 64 and 67. There are resonances here to the Sanskrit concept of *pitha*, a material work that can function as the "seat" or "bench" for a presencing of divinity. For further discussion, see Diana L. Eck, *Banaras: City of Light* (New York: Knopf, 1982).

55. Ventura, "Chronology," 64 and 67.
56. "Lynn Tillman in Conversation with Kiki Smith," 40.
57. Heidegger's correspondence with his brother Fritz, a substantial selection of which is reproduced in Walter Homolka and Arnulf Heidegger, eds., *Heidegger und der Antisemismus: Positionen im Widerstreit, mit Briefen von Martin und Fritz Heidegger* (Freiburg: Herder, 2016), 326–341, attests to the complexity, ranging from the empirical to the esoteric, of his understanding of *Heimat*.
58. Hermann Schmitz, "Heidegger und der Nationalsozialismus," in *Heidegger und der Antisemismus*, 326–341.
59. See Schmitz, "Heidegger und der Nationalsozialismus," 339.
60. Heidegger, "Der Ursprung des Kunstwerkes," 54.
61. Martin Heidegger, *Die Grundbegriffe der Metaphysik: Welt–Endlichkeit–Einsamkeit*, ed. Friedrich-Wilhelm von Herrmann, Heidegger Gesamtausgabe (GA) 29–30 (Frankfurt: Klostermann, 1983). English translation by William McNeill and Nicholas Walker, *The Fundamental Concepts of Metaphysics: World, Finitude, Solitude* (Bloomington: Indiana University Press, 1995).
62. For more detailed discussion and references, see my *Tracing Expression in Merleau-Ponty*, chap. 4.
63. *White Mice with Ruby Eyes*, 1999, painted bronze and rubies. Thirty-three units; installation dimensions variable. Collection of the artist.
64. David George Haskell, *The Forest Unseen: A Year's Watch in Nature* (New York: Viking, 2012), 236–238.
65. Johnson, *The Retrieval of the Beautiful*, 224.
66. Johnson, *The Retrieval of the Beautiful*, 228.
67. Johnson, *The Retrieval of the Beautiful*, 228.
68. Smith, as quoted by Ventura, "Chronology," 56–97.
69. "Lynn Tillman in Conversation with Kiki Smith," 40.
70. "Lynn Tillman in Conversation with Kiki Smith," 41.
71. See here Emmanuel Alloa, "The Diacritical Nature of Meaning: Merleau-Ponty with Saussure," *Chiasmi* 15 (2013): 167–168. Johnson's "laceworks," together with Merleau-Ponty's emphasis on gaps, lacunae, or *écart*, need ultimately to be interpreted in the context of his engagement with diacritics and Saussurean linguistics. However, Kearney's argument (see note 72) restrains this emphasis on diacritics.
72. Richard Kearney, "Écrire la chair: l'expression diacritique chez Merleau-Ponty," *Chiasmi* 15 (2013): 1183–1196. The quotations are from section 4, 190–193.
73. VI, 195; 149.
74. VI, 197; 115.
75. Siri Engberg, "Introduction: Making Things," in *Kiki Smith: A Gathering, 1980–2005*, 18–29; 19.

76. OE, 71–72; EM, 373. Merleau-Ponty's specific reference is to the sculpture of Henry Moore.
77. *Revelation*, 1994. Ink on Nepalese paper and papier-mâché; figure, 12 × 67 × 15 in., installation dimensions variable. Collection of Eileen Harris Norton and Peter Norton.
78. *Dewbow*, 1999. Fumed glass, 206 units (ranging in size from 51.4 to 9 in.), installation dimensions variable. Collection of the National Museum of Art, Osaka, Japan.
79. *Paradise Cage*, 1997. Installation in cooperation with Wolf D. Prix of Vienna's Co-op Himmelblau. Installation dimensions variable. Collection of the Museum of Contemporary Art, Los Angeles.
80. OE, 70; EM, 371.
81. OE, 86; EM, 376.

Chapter 3

1. "Eye and Mind," written in the summer of 1960, at Le Tholonet, near Aix-en-Provence, and thus in daily contact with the landscapes that inspired Cézanne and that were natal to him, was commissioned for and first published in *Art de France* in January 1961. Claude Lefort comments, in his preface to *L'œil et l'esprit*, that the landscape that Merleau-Ponty's text evokes is one "where the nearby diffuses itself into the distant, and the distant makes the nearby vibrate, [and] where the presence of things gives itself on a ground of absence, where being and appearing [*l'apparence*] are interchanged." OE, iv.
2. OE, 13; EM, 352. One needs to keep in mind that Merleau-Ponty is not expressing reservations concerning science as such (he was, indeed, a passionate reader and informed discussant of science, especially of psychology and biology), but rather he is critical of a certain conception and practice of scientific thinking.
3. OE, 13–14; EM, 353.
4. Maurice Merleau-Ponty, "Le langage indirect et les voix du silence," in *Signes* (Paris: Gallimard, 1960), 63–153. English translation by Richard C. McCleary, "Indirect Language and the Voices of Silence," in *Signs* (Evanston: Northwestern University Press, 1964), 39–83.
5. "Le langage indirect," *Signes* (Paris: Gallimard, 1969), 69–135.
6. Maurice Merleau-Ponty, *Notes de cours, 1959–1961* (Paris: Gallimard, 1996).
7. Merleau-Ponty, *Notes de cours*, 183.
8. Merleau-Ponty, *Notes de cours*, 183. On the notion of *voyance*, derived from Rimbaud, see Carbone, *The Flesh of Images*, 3, 30–37.
9. Kaushik, *Art, Language, and Figure in Merleau-Ponty*.

10. Kirk Varnedoe, "Inscriptions in Arcadia," in *Cy Twombly: A Retrospective* (New York: Harry N. Abrams, 1994), 10.

11. See Roland Barthes, *The Responsibility of Forms: Critical Essays on Music, Art, and Representation*, trans. Richard Howard (New York: Hill and Wang, 1985).

12. Mary Jacobus, *Reading Cy Twombly: Poetry in Paint* (Princeton: Princeton University Press, 2016). See in particular her "Introduction: Twombly's Books," but also the detailed analyses that she, having access to Twombly's own marked-up books, offers in subsequent chapters.

13. Kaushik, *Art, Language, and Figure in Merleau-Ponty*, chap. 4.

14. Yves Michaud, "Joan Mitchell: Abstract Expressionism and Feeling," exhibition catalogue *Kunsthalle Emden*, as cited by Michelle Yun, "Zao Wou-Ki and the Avant-Garde," in Melissa Walt, Ankeney Weitz, and Michelle Yun, *No Limits: Zao Wou-Ki* (New York and Waterville: Asia Society Museum and Colby College of Art, 2016), 50.

15. Jacobus, *Reading Cy Twombly*, 19.

16. See Varnedoe, "Inscriptions in Arcadia," 41–42.

17. This remark introduces section 2 of "Eye and Mind." It must obviously not be understood prosaically in the sense that painting is a bodily labor. Nonetheless, it is of some relevance that the execution of these works, in oil crayon on wet house paint, required a sort of athleticism as well as bodily collaboration, with Twombly sitting on the shoulders of his collaborator and partner, Nicola del Roscio, to paint the panels' upper reaches. Joan Mitchell, faced with a similar difficulty of access, used ladders, even when her double hip replacement made both ascending and descending them excruciating.

18. For discussion, see chap. 4.

19. VI, 195–198. The quotations are from 195.

20. Nicholas Cullinan, "Mourning and Melancholia: *Nini's Paintings*," in *Cy Twombly: Cycles and Seasons*, ed. Nicholas Serota (London: Tate, 2008), 137.

21. Cullinan, "Mourning and Melancholia," 138–139.

22. OE, 21; EM, 355.

23. Roland Barthes, "Cy Twombly ou 'Non multa sed multum,'" in *Cy Twombly: Cinquante années de dessin*, ed. Jonas Storsve and Simon Schama (Paris: Éditions Gallimard / Centre Pompidou, 2004), 37–42. Though this is incidental, it is nonetheless interesting that Barthes himself was left-handed, and that "left" is the basic meaning of *gauche*. It is also interesting that both Twombly and Ellsworth Kelly served in the army as cryptographers and privately practiced drawing without conscious or ocular control. On Kelly, see chap. 5 in this volume. In this context, see also Richard Shiff's comment in his "Charm," in *Cy Twombly: Cycles and Seasons*, ed. Nicholas Serota (London: Tate, 2008), 27, that with Twombly's sightless graphic trait, meaning came to derive "from a manual act of writing that created its own signs, a handwriting that functioned as a mode of drawing."

24. OE, 81; EM, 374. Joan Mitchell who, like Twombly, was generally averse to talking about her art, nonetheless stressed such "absence" from self as important to and characteristic of her best work.

25. Tacita Dean, "A Panegyric," in *Cy Twombly: Cycles and Seasons*, ed. Nicholas Serota (London: Tate, 2008), 36, my emphasis. The titles of some of Twombly's relevant works were assigned to them purely by chance from a list drawn up by Robert Rauschenberg and Jasper Johns.

26. On the role of the rhapsode in relation to the Homeric epics, see Plato's short dialogue, *Ion*.

27. Dean, "A Panegyric," 35.

28. See Jacques Derrida, *Of Grammatology*, trans. Gayatri Spivak (Baltimore: Johns Hopkins University Press, 2016).

29. Nicholas Cullinan, "American-Type Painting," in *Cy Twombly: Cycles and Seasons*, ed. Nicholas Serota (London: Tate, 2008), 58. In this context, see also Jean-Pierre Basquiat's acknowledgment that Twombly "really cancels" by his erasures, whereas Basquiat himself "cancels to reveal," in Robert Farris Thomson, *Aesthetics of the Cool: Afro Atlantic Art and* Music (New York: Periscope, 2011), 83.

30. Institution is understood here in the sense that Merleau-Ponty gives it, as a synonym for the Husserlian notion of *Urstiftung*, in his 1954–1955 lecture course. See *L'institution dans l'histoire personnelle et publique: Le problème de la passivité, le sommeil, l'inconscient, la mémoire: Notes de cours au Collège de France*, ed. Dominique Darmaillacq, Claude Lefort, and Stéphanie Ménasé (Paris: Éditions Belin, 2003).The obliterated is not understood here in the sense of the catastrophically destroyed, such as Herculaneum and Pompeii (of which the traces remain vivid and wrenching), even though, as it happens, Cullinan explores Twombly's relation to "the presence of death in the present," referring to Freud's study of the "Pompeiian Fancy" of a novella by Wilhelm Jensen, in *Sigmund Freud: Delusions and Dreams in Jensen's Gradiva*, ed. and trans. James Strachey, *Standard Edition of the Complete Psychological Works of Sigmund Freud* (London: Hogarth Press, 1954–1975), vol. 9, 7–93. Merleau-Ponty examines the Freudian text in the section of the *Institution* lectures that treat of "The Problem of Passivity: Sleep, the Unconscious, Memory" (*L'institution*, 157–258).

31. Working Note of November 1959, VI, 269; 215. *Nichturpräsentierbar* (incapable of originary presentation) is a Husserlian term to which Merleau-Ponty frequently resorts.

32. Both paintings are oil pastel, lead pencil, and collage on paper, 150 × 135 cm. Twombly's penchant for pairing works seems to reflect his early interest in symmetry, which he took to be characteristic of both aboriginal and classical art, interlinking them.

33. Heidegger, "Der Ursprung des Kunstwerkes," 31.

34. Heidegger, "Der Ursprung des Kunstwerkes," 33.

35. Heidegger, "Der Ursprung des Kunstwerkes," 30.

36. Concerning Heidegger's understanding of the German people's destinal mandate, see the documentation and interpretive essay s in Homolka and Heidegger, *Heidegger und der Antisemitismus*. The book also and importantly contains much of Heidegger's correspondence with his brother Fritz.

37. Cullinan, "American-Type Painting," 83.

38. Jacobus, *Reading Cy Twombly*, 72.

39. See Cullinan, "American-Type Painting," 85.

40. Jacobus, *Reading Cy Twombly*, 72.

41. Cullinan, "American-Type Painting," 101. On the roles of scatological defilement, see Michel Serres, *Malfeasance*, trans. Anne-Marie Feenberg-Dibon (Stanford: Stanford University Press, 2011).

42. See PhP, 162–163, 171.

43. PhP, 174.

44. Kaushik, *Art, Language, and Figuration in Merleau-Ponty*, 129.

45. Kaushik, *Art, Language, and Figuration in Merleau-Ponty*, 131.

46. Both are oil paint, wax crayon, pencil, and collage, 55.875 × 50.75 in. (142 × 128 cm.). Private collection.

47. The Egyptian lotus (actually a tropical water lily, *Nymphaea caerulea*) was symbolic of rejuvenation and rebirth. It also appears in an untitled 1977 sculpture by Twombly, in which three lotus flower forms are borne aloft on a kind of chariot.

48. Jacobus, *Reading Cy Twombly*, 105.

49. See Joshua Rivkin, *Chalk: The Art and Erasure of Cy Twombly* (Brooklyn: Melville House, 2018). See chap. 27, "Epitaph," in particular, 263. Of course, an artist is not constrained by but can counteract his natural inclination.

50. OE, 13–15; EM, 352–353.

51. The *Lepanto* series is titled after the 1571 naval battle between the victorious "Holy League" and the Ottoman Empire. In his tape-recorded interview with Nicholas Serota of September and December 2007, Twombly characterizes the series as one of the "good moments" he experienced as an artist. He speaks about "these reds . . . that strange lobster color," and about "making the boats." See Cy Twombly and Nicholas Serota, "History Behind the Thought," *Cy Twombly: Cycles and Seasons*, ed. Nicholas Serota (London: Tate, 2008), 53.

52. Jacobus, *Reading Cy Twombly*, 108. Jacobus also points out that the association with rocketry is significant, given the spectacular and environmentally damaging nuclear tests that were carried out during this period.

53. Twombly and Serota, "History Behind the Thought," 45.

54. Varnedoe, "Inscriptions in Arcadia," 45. Twombly's reference in *Discourses on Commodus is* to the second-century Roman emperor Lucius Aurelius Commodus, whose deranged mind and persona proved disastrous for the empire.

55. Jacobus, *Reading Cy Twombly*, 124.

56. Jacobus, *Reading Cy Twombly*, 221.
57. See Plato, *Republic*, X.
58. OE, 62; EM, 368.
59. The main dissenting voice is again Rivkin's.
60. *Thicket*, 1991. Wood, white cement, paper, wooden tags, and paint, 160 × 41 × 41 cm. Estate of Cy Twombly. See Cullinan, "American-Type Painting," 195–196, and Jeremy Lewison, *Turner, Monet, Twombly: Later Paintings* (London: Tate, 2012), 22–23.
61. Jacobus, *Reading Cy Twombly*, 129.
62. *Epitaph*, 1992. Wood, plaster, plywood, paint, 15.812 × 15.5 × 15.5 in. (40.2 × 39.4 × 38.7 cm.). Menil Collection. Rivkin takes "Epitaph" as the title of his short chapter disagreeing with Jacobus and with kindred interpretations.
63. Jacobus, *Reading Cy Twombly*, 132.
64. Lewison, *Turner, Monet, Twombly*, 22.
65. For details of chronology and circumstances, see Nela Pavlouskova, *Cy Twombly: Late Paintings, 2003–2011*, trans. David H. Wilson (London: Thames and Hudson, 2015), 36–47. See also A. Heinrich, "Dionysos," in *The Oxford Classical Dictionary*, 4th ed. (Oxford: Oxford University Press, 2012), 461–464.
66. Jacobus, *Reading Cy Twombly*, 132.
67. OE, 79; EM, 373–374.
68. Maurice Merleau-Ponty, "The Film and the New Psychology," in *Sense and Non-Sense*, trans. Hubert L. Dreyfus and Patricia Allen Dreyfus (Evanston: Northwestern University Press, 1991), 48–59.
69. See Carbone, *The Flesh of Images*, 54; and Merleau-Ponty, *Sense and Non-Sense*, 54.
70. Merleau-Ponty, *Sense and Non-Sense*, 58–59.
71. Carbone, *The Flesh of Images*, 52. Anna Caterina Dalmasso offers a thoughtful and well-informed discussion of these issues in her *Le corps, c'est l'écran*. See in particular chap. 1, section 3.
72. Merleau-Ponty, *Nature*, 167–199. For discussion, see my *Tracing Expression in Merleau-Ponty*, chap.4. I now think that the part-whole relation is as fundamental to Merleau-Ponty's thought as is expression.
73. VI, 183–184; 139.
74. Renaud Barbaras, "L'autonomie de l'apparaître," *Chiasmi* 15 (2014): 27–35. This study does not, however, espouse Barbaras's view that hyper-belonging proves to be incompatible with the ontology of flesh.
75. Emmanuel de Saint Aubert, in "Conscience et expression chez Merleau-Ponty," *Chiasmi* 10 (2008): 85–106, notes that Merleau-Ponty's 1953 course at the Collège de France, The Sensible World and the World of Expression, is the first Merleau-Pontian text to highlight the notion of *écart*.
76. Dean, "A Panegyric," 40.

77. Dean, "A Panegyric," 41.

78. *Poems to the Sea*, suite of twenty-four works, 1959. Oil, graphite, and wax crayon on paper, 32.4 × 31.1 cm. Dia Art Foundation. *Hero and Leandro*, 1981–1984, four parts. Crayon and graphite on canvas, and crayon and graphite on graph paper (part 4), dimensions variable. Daros Collection, Switzerland. *Hero and Leandro (to Christopher Marlowe)*, 1985. Oil and oil-based house paint on canvas, 79.5 × 100 in. (102 × 254 cm.). Estate of Cy Twombly. *Untitled (A Painting in Nine Parts)*, 1988. Oil, water-based paint, graphite, and metallic paint on wood panel. Formats and dimensions variable. The Menil Collection.

79. *Leaving Paphos Ringed with Waves*, four parts, 2009. Acrylic on canvas, 267.4 × 22.3 × 35 cm. (105.25 × 8.375 × 13.5 in.). Cy Twombly Foundation. Consider also Twombly's *Gaeta Set (For the Love of Fire and Water)* of 1981. The ten drawings (in oil and pastel on paper) comprising this set were paired with Octavio Paz's poetry to create an artist's book. See Jacobus, "Postscript: Writing in Light," *Reading Cy Twombly*, 234–241. The works are in the collection of Udo and Annette Brandhorst and the Cy Twombly Foundation.

80. *Octavio Paz, Eight Poems / Cy Twombly, Ten Drawings* (Cologne: Udo and Annette Brandhorst, 1991). For discussion, see Jacobus, "Postscript: Writing in Light," *Reading Cy Twombly*.

81. For discussion of Twombly's attentiveness to plant life, see Jacobus, *Reading Cy Twombly*, chap. 6.

82. For the peonies and haiku, see Cy Twombly, *Untitled*, 2007. Acrylic, wax crayon, and lead pencil on wooden panel, 99.25 × 217.25 in. (252 × 552 cm.). Collection of Donald B. and Catherine C. Marron, New York. For the late rose images, see Cy Twombly, *The Rose*, five parts, 2008. Acrylic on wooden panels, 99.25 × 229.375 in. (252 × 740 cm.). Gagosian Gallery / Cy Twombly Foundation.

83. Nicholas Cullinan, "Between Roses and Shadows," citing T. S. Eliot, "Little Gidding," in *Four Quartets*, 1943, in *Cy Twombly: Cycles and Seasons*, ed. Nicholas Serota (London: Tate, 2008), 241.

84. Kaushik, *Art, Language, and Figure in Merleau-Ponty*, 1–18.

85. I am basing my reading of the fragment on Jean Bollack and Heinz Wismann's text in *Héraclite ou la séparation* (Paris: Éditions de Minuit, 1972).

86. Jacobus quotes from a collaborative artist's book, *Octavio Paz, Eight Poems / Cy Twombly, Ten Drawings* (Cologne: Udo and Annette Brandhorst, 1993). Neither the poems nor the art (Twombly's *Gaeta Set*) had any connection with each other to begin with but came to complement each other. Paz himself speaks of seeing "the invisible in some ways." For discussion see Jacobus, *Reading Cy Twombly*, 237.

Chapter 4

1. For discussion, see Carbone, *The Flesh of Images*, 31–33.

2. Claude Lefort, "Préface" to Maurice Merleau-Ponty, *Notes de cours, 1959–1961*, ed. Stéphanie Ménasé (Paris: Gallimard, 1996), 21, cited hereafter by the abbreviation NC. The link between silence, always important to Mitchell, and nonfigurative painting deserves exploration.

3. Carbone, *The Flesh of Images*, 38.

4. See Claude Simon, *L'Herbe* (Paris: Éditions de Minuit, 1958), together with Alastair B. Duncan's excellent essay (in the same volume, 187–202), "Lire *L'Herbe*."

5. Yves Michaud, "Entretiens," January 12, 1986, in *Joan Mitchell*, ed. Françoise Bonnefoy (Paris: Éditions du Jeu de Paume, 1994), 19.

6. Maurice Merleau-Ponty, "La philosophie aujourd'hui: cours de 1958–1959," in NC, 54.

7. NC, 54.

8. See Judith Bernstock, *Joan Mitchell* (New York: Hudson Hills Press, 1988), 121–122, who links Mitchell's relation to nature to Baudelaire and Beckett.

9. I explore aspects of Mitchell's relation to Monet, and both artists' resilience, in their art, to personal losses and trauma in my "Adversity and Practices of Painting: Merleau-Ponty and Joan Mitchell," *Philosophy Today* 60, no. 2 (2016): 397–405.

10. See here Carbone, *The Flesh of Images*, 60. Carbone links such a past to an "active oblivion" that distills carnal essences.

11. Michaud, "Entretiens," 27.

12. Klaus Kertess, *Joan Mitchell* (New York: Harry N. Abrams, 1997), 20.

13. Linda Nochlin, "Joan Mitchell: A Rage to Paint," in *The Paintings of Joan Mitchell*, ed. Jane Livingston (New York and Berkeley: The Whitney Museum of American Art and University of California Press, 2002), 49–60; 55.

14. One needs, however, to keep in mind here Anna Caterina Dalmasso's characterization of the figure/ground relation, for Merleau-Ponty, as encompassing "a ground of invisibility," and of a "negativity that makes its way through the sensible and is the catalyst for the production of a sense always in excess of it." See her *Le corps c'est l'écran*, 21. See also 37. The publication of the book succeeded the completion of this work.

15. Bernstock, *Joan Mitchell*, 34.

16. Jane Livingston, "The Paintings of Joan Mitchell," in *The Paintings of Joan Mitchell*, ed. Jane Livingston, with essays by Linda Nochlin, Yvetter Y. Lee, and Jane Livingston (Berkeley: University of California Press, 2002), 40.

17. Kertess, *Joan Mitchell*, 33.

18. Michaud, "Entretiens," 26. Mitchell goes on to affirm that "when I paint, I am not conscious of myself . . . the painting tells me what needs to be done. It is not at all a part of myself . . ." (27; my translation).

19. OE, 67; EM, 71.

20. Michaud, "Entretiens," August 7, 1989, 29.

21. Bonnefoy, *Joan Mitchell*, 31.

22. Bernstock, *Joan Mitchell*, 29.

23. The full title of the former painting is *George Went Swimming at Barnes Hole but It Got Too Cold*. George was her French poodle who died that year. *To the Harbormaster* was titled after a poem by Frank O'Hara.

24. Marion was one of the puppies born to Mitchell's German shepherd, Iva.

25. "Peindre, c'est une maniére de se sentir 'vivre,'" interview with Michaud, January 12, 1986, 26.

26. Kertess, *Joan Mitchell*, 39.

27. OE, 68; EM, 370.

28. OE, 69; EM, 370.

29. Concerning the autofigure, see Kaushik, *Art, Language, and Figure in Merleau-Ponty*. Kaushik understands the autofigure as being's inability to "enact itself" without being figured forth into appearances.

30. See her interview with Michaud of January 12, 1986, which opens with a discussion of her experiences of illness and hospitalization.

31. Bernstock, *Joan Mitchell*, 79.

32. See Bernstock, *Joan Mitchell*, 51.

33. Nochlin, "Joan Mitchell: A Rage to Paint," 58.

34. Carbone, *The Flesh of Images*, 72.

35. OE, 63; EM, 368.

36. Interview with Michaud, January 12, 1986, 25. She tells Michaud that she will remember him, by virtue of her "enframing," as she sees him now, changelessly: "you are alive and I am alive, of a single piece" (25).

37. Bernstock, *Joan Mitchell*, 46.

38. NC, 200.

39. NC, 211.

40. NC, 211. The phrasing is Simon's, and the reference is to Simon's novel *Le vent* (The wind), in which a woman's death leaves her son, who survives her, older than she was, thus bringing about a change in his duration.

41. Plato, *Republic*, 387d–e, 603e–605a. This ideal self-sufficiency contrasts sharply with Homer's *Iliad*, which shows Achilles to be so moved by Priam's mourning for his son Hector (whom Achilles had slain) that he desists from enacting vengeance by abusing Hector's corpse.

42. Michaud, interview of January 12, 1986.

43. Yvette Y. Lee, in "Beyond Life and Death: Joan Mitchell's *Grand e Vallée* Suite," in *The Paintings of Joan Mitchell*, ed. Jane Livingston (New York and Berkeley: The Whitney Museum of American Art and University of California Press, 2002), 61–74, quotes Barreau to the effect that "painting is like music—it is beyond life and death. It is another dimension" (65).

44. Kertess, *Joan Mitchell*, 41.

45. *Joan Mitchell: An Exhibition of Paintings*, curated by John Cheim. New York: Robert Miller Gallery, October 25 to November 25, 1989.

46. Michaud, interview of January 12, 1986, 26.

47. VI, 164; 123.
48. VI, 165; 124.
49. VI, 271; 218. See also the reference to *partie totale* (total part) in OE, 17; EM, 354.
50. VI, 274; 218.
51. VI, 195–200; 149–153.
52. VI 197; 150.
53. VI, 196; 149. Merleau-Ponty's quotation marks.
54. The late abstract painter Peter Pinchbeck liked to call it "corporate art" (personal communication).
55. *Mountain*, diptych, 1989. Oil on canvas, 110.25 × 157.5. Estate of Joan Mitchell.
56. "Le peintre 'apporte son corps,'" OE, 16; EM, 353. "The painter takes his body with him," which seems to be the accepted translation, is both clumsy and misleading (not to mention its implicit sexism).
57. For discussion, see Carbone, *The Flesh of Images*, 10–12.
58. *Weather*, 1989. Oil on canvas, 51.5 × 32 in. Estate of Joan Mitchell.
59. VI, 271–272; 217–219. I translate the genitive literally, rather than as "Being in indivision."
60. VI, 299–300; 246.
61. VI, 299; 246.

Chapter 5

1. OE, 87; EM, 376.
2. A reproduction of *Hyacinth*, 1949 (16.5 × 12 in.), appears, among other places, in Richard H. Axsom, *Drawn from Nature: The Plant Lithographs of Ellsworth Kelly* (New Haven: Yale University Press, 2005), 13.
3. Ellsworth Kelly, "Notes of 1969," in Kristine Stiles and Peter Selz, eds., *Theories and Documents of Contemporary Art: A Sourcebook of Artists' Writings*, ed. Kristine Stiles and Peter Selz, 2nd rev. and expanded edition by Kristine Selz (Berkeley: University of California Press, 2012), 119.
4. *Wesen*, understood verbally, may be paraphrased as what prevails (*west*) or holds sway.
5. OE, 84; EM, 375.
6. OE, 85; EM, 375.
7. See here Rachel Cooke, "Ellsworth Kelly: I Want to Live Another 15 Years," Interview, November 6, 2015, *The Guardian*, US edition, November 8, 2015 (unpaginated). Accessed January 16, 2016, at *the guardian.com/US*. Kelly died December 28, 2015.
8. OE, 90; EM, 377.

9. Robert Storr, "Starting Out—Starting Over," in *Ellsworth Kelly*, ed. Tricia Y. Paik (London: Phaidon Press, 2015), 88–103; 89.

10. Storr, "Starting Out—Starting Over," 92. Beckmann's lecture was entitled "Letters to a Woman Painter" and is published in Max Beckmann, *On My Painting* (Madras: Hanuman Books, 1988). I cite the statement as quoted by Storr.

11. Quoted by Tricia Y. Paik in her chapter, "In New York, 1954–70," in *Ellsworth Kelly* (London: Phaidon Press, 2015), 115, with reference to Charles Hagen, "The Shape of Seeing: Ellsworth Kelly's Photographs," *Aperture* 125 (Fall 1991). Understanding Kelly's claim to non-invention is a guiding theme of Paik's research.

12. Quoted by Storr, "Starting Out—Starting Over," 91; he supplies the date of this remark, presumably communicated privately, on 93.

13. Cited by Rémi Labrusse in "Le désir de la ligne," in *Henri Matisse—Ellsworth Kelly: Dessins de Plantes*, ed. Agnès de la Beaumelle (Paris: Gallimard/Centre Pompidou, 2002), 45. Translations from the French are mine.

14. Eric de Chassey, "Aller avec . . . ," in *Henri Matisse—Ellsworth Kelly: Dessins de Plantes*, ed. Agnès de la Beaumelle (Paris: Gallimard/Centre Pompidou, 2002), 67, 68. De Chassey quotes Matisse's statement in a letter of June 1943: "One must not work with elements of nature that have not passed through feeling [*le sentiment*]" (67).

15. Axsom, *Drawn from Nature*, 13.

16. They were shown as part of the exhibition *New York Painting and Sculpture, 1940–1970* at the Metropolitan Museum of Art. For details, see Paik, *Ellsworth Kelly*, 124.

17. Formats range from approximately 35 × 25 in. to approximately 39 × 47 in.

18. For an informative discussion of transfer lithography and of Kelly's choices of paper and his collaboration with presses and master printers, see Axsom, *Drawn from Nature*, 14–17. A full technical discussion of lithography can be found in Ralph Mayer, *The Artist's Handbook of Materials and Techniques*, 3rd rev. ed. (New York: Viking Press, 1970), 574–584.

19. Axsom, *Drawn from Nature*, 17. In 1950, Kelly created *Automatic Drawing: Pine Branches, I–VII*. Concerning a similar practice that Twombly adopted, see chap. 3.

20. OE, 25; EM, 356.

21. OE, 18–19; EM, 354. The feminine gender, which I here introduce, is absent from Merleau-Ponty's analyses of painting.

22. OE, 22–23; EM, 355.

23. Axsom, *Drawn from Nature*, 21.

24. Axsom, *Drawn from Nature*, 17.

25. VI, 174; 132.

26. Gavin Delahunty, "Memory Recorded and Transferred," in Tricia Y. Paik, *Ellsworth Kelly* (London: Phaidon, 2015), 182–187; 185.

27. Axsom, *Drawn from Nature*, 16–17. *Catalpa Leaf* is part of the series *Suite of Plant Lithographs* (1964–1966).

28. *Colors for a Large Wall*, 1951. Oil on canvas. Sixty-four conjoined panels, 240 × 240 cm. New York, Museum of Modern Art.
29. Quoted by Paik, *Ellsworth Kelly*, 39.
30. In contrast, the penciled lines defining Agnes Martin's mathematical grids still convey the energy of her hand. Kelly maintained a close friendship with Martin during the time they both lived at Coenties Slip.
31. *Spectrum I*, 1953. Oil on canvas, 60.25 × 60.25 in (153 × 153 cm.). Museum of Modern Art and the Helen and Charles Schwab Collection.
32. Paik uses this terminology throughout her essay "In New York City, 1954–70," in *Ellsworth Kelly*, 107–125.
33. Paik, *Ellsworth Kelly*, 125.
34. *Spectrum V*, 1969. Oil on canvas, thirteen panels, 64 × 588 in. (213.4 × 1,493.5 cm.). The Metropolitan Museum of Art, New York.
35. OE, 76; EM, 373.
36. The reference is to *La Combe I–IV* of 1950–1951, *Meschers* of 1951, and to *Atlantic* of 1956.
37. OE, 29; EM, 357.
38. Kelly, "Notes of 1969," 118.
39. Kelly, "Notes of 1969."
40. *Black Ripe*, 1955. Oil on canvas, 63.25 × 59.375 in. (160.7 × 150.8 cm.). The Anderson Collection at Stanford University. *Red Blue*, 1964. Oil on canvas, 90 × 66 in. (228.6 × 167.6 cm.). Thomas H. Lee and Ann Tenenbaum collection.
41. *Sculpture for a Large Wall*, 1957. Polished and anodized aluminum, 138 × 785 × 13 in.; 3.5 × 19.9 × 0.3 m. Museum of Modern Art, New York.
42. Paik, Ellsworth *Kelly*, 121.
43. Axsom, *Drawn from Nature*, 17.
44. See, for instance, *Curve X*, 1974. Weathering steel, 120 × 16 × 0.75 in. (304.8 × 50.8 × 1.9 cm.), Harvard Art Museums, and *Totem (for Roy Lichtenstein)*, 1998. Bronze, 168 × 28 × 1.25 in. (426.7 × 71.1 × 3.2 cm.). Fondation Hubert Looser, Zurich.
45. Kelly, "Notes of 1969," 119.
46. OE, 47; EM, 363.
47. *Black Curves*, 1954. Oil on canvas, 30 × 26 in. (91.4 × 66 cm.). Collection of the artist.
48. Delahunty, "Memory Recorded," 182.
49. Delahunty, "Memory Recorded," 182. Delahunty's reference is to Henry Geldzahler, "Ellsworth Kelly," in *Toward a New Abstraction* (New York: The Jewish Museum, 1953), 16.
50. Gary Garrels, "Painting and Architecture," in Tricia Y. Paik, *Ellsworth Kelly* (London: Phaidon, 2015), 322–329; 327.
51. OE, 25; EM, 356.
52. OE, 71; EM, 371.

53. See M. H. Miller, "A Temple for Light," with photographs by Victoria Sambunaris, *The New York Times Style Magazine*, February 18, 2018, 218–223.
54. OE, 76; EM, 372, and OE, 87; EM, 376.
55. OE, 87; EM, 376.
56. See Dürer's *Das grosse Rasenstück*, watercolor and body color on vellum, Graphische Sammlung, Albertina, Vienna; and Leonardo's *Blackberries*, red chalk, pen, and white pigment on tinted paper, The Royal Collection, London.
57. Kelly, "Notes of 1969," 119. The early American reception of his art, though livelier than the French, tended to assimilate his work superficially to the heritage of Mondrian.
58. Shirley Sherwood, *A Passion for Plants: Contemporary Botanical Masterworks* (London: Cassell & Co., 2001), 15.
59. McEwen's earlier series, *True Facts from Nature*, focusing on dead leaves and other vegetal debris, includes a painting, *Northern Leaves for Cy, 1973*, that was given to Cy Twombly in exchange for a drawing.
60. Labrusse, "Le désir de la ligne," 17–49. Labrusse does not mention Merleau-Ponty, but he cites Valéry's phrase that "les choses nous regardent [things look at us]," which is among Merleau-Ponty's inspirations.
61. Labrusse, "Le désir de la ligne," 30.
62. OE, 72–74; EM, 371–372.
63. Merleau-Ponty, "Cézanne's Doubt," 16.
64. Merleau-Ponty, *La nature*. Citations are to the translation, which is referred to as N.
65. Maurice Merleau-Ponty, *The Structure of Behavior*, trans. Alden L. Fisher (Pittsburgh: Duquesne University Press, 2008). The work was originally published in 1942. See George E. Coghill, *Anatomy and the Problem of Behavior* (Cambridge: Cambridge University Press, 1929). Contrary to the prevalent classification of Amblysoma as a lizard, David Morris identifies it as a salamander. See his *Merleau-Ponty's Developmental Ontology* (Evanston: Northwestern University Press, 2018), 212.
66. N, 140.
67. N, 143.
68. See Michael Pollan, "The Intelligent Plant: Scientists Debate a New Way to Understand Flora," *The New Yorker*, December 23 and 30, 2013, 92–105.
69. Patricia M. Locke, "Intimate Intertwining: A Merleau-Pontian Account of My Microbiota, and Me," *Chiasmi* 18 (2016): 247–259; 247.
70. N, 197.
71. N, 177.
72. N, 176.
73. See Merlin Tuttle, *The Secret Lives of Bats* (New York: Houghton Mifflin, 2018), chaps. 8 and 12.
74. Heidegger, *Die Grundbegriffe der Metaphysik*, 293. English translation by McNeill and Walker, *The Fundamental Concepts of Metaphysics*.

75. N, 120.
76. N, 114.
77. N, 121.
78. Waldenfels, "Going and Coming of Time," 234.
79. I leave out of consideration here the scholarly question of what Anaximander's genuine words may be as distinguished from later accretions, in particular Heidegger's textual "surgery" on the fragment in "Der Spruch des Anaximander" (The saying of Anaximander) in *Holzwege*, 296–343. Heidegger eliminates the phrase *kata tēn tou khronou taxin* (in keeping with the order of time) from the genuine Anaximandrian text.
80. *Burdock*, 1986. Pencil on paper, 13 × 10 in. Staatliche graphsche Sammlung, Munich.

Chapter 6

1. Jean-Luc Nancy, "Forbidden Representation," *The Ground of the Image*, trans. Jeff Fort (New York: Fordham University Press, 2005), 35.
2. Nancy, "Forbidden Representation," 38.
3. Nancy, "Forbidden Representation," 38.
4. Johnson, *The Retrieval of the Beautiful*, 5, 10.
5. Martin Heidegger, *Besinnung*, ed. Friedrich-Wilhelm von Herrmann, *Heidegger Gesamtausgabe* (GA) 66, 30, 34. Translations from both German and French are mine unless otherwise indicated.
6. Neal Benezra, "The Misadventures of Beauty," in *Regarding Beauty: A View of the Late Twentieth Century*, ed. Neal Benezra and Olga M. Viso (Washington, DC: Hirshhorn Museum and Sculpture Garden, with Hatje Cantz Publishers, 1999), 16–38. See 28.
7. François Cheng, *Fünf Meditationen über die Schönheit*, trans. Judith Klein (Munich: C. H. Beck, 2009), 18. The volume was originally published as *Cinq Méditations sur la beauté* (Paris: Éditions Albin Michel, 2006). I translate from the German.
8. *Causeries* has been translated into English as *The World of Perception* by Oliver Davis (London: Routledge, 2004). See section 6.
9. Maurice Merleau-Ponty, *L'ontologie cartésienne et l'ontologie d'aujourd'hui*, cours de 1960–1961, in Stéphanie Ménasé, ed., *Maurice Merleau-Ponty, Notes des cours au Collège de France, 1958–1959. and 1960–1961* (Paris: Gallimard, 1996), 205. This statement forms the epigraph of chapter 4.
10. OE, 31; EM, 358.
11. Johnson, *The Retrieval of the Beautiful*, 80–85. Johnson, who uses and perhaps coins the expression "strong beauty," understands it in a sense close to Rodin's incorporating what is commonly considered ugly or unworthy of artistic

representation in his understanding of beauty. I am seeking here an understanding that is both more encompassing and more ethically oriented.

12. Olga M. Viso, "Beauty and Its Dilemmas," in *Regarding Beauty: A View of the Late Twentieth Century*, ed. Neal Benezra and Olga M. Viso (Washington, DC: Hirshhorn Museum and Sculpture Garden, with Hatje Cantz Publishers, 1999), 83–133; see 97–101.

13. Arthur C. Danto, "Beauty for Ashes," in *Regarding Beauty: A View of the Late Twentieth Century*, ed. Neal Benezra and Olga M. Viso (Washington, DC: Hirshhorn Museum and Sculpture Garden, with Hatje Cantz Publishers, 1999), 182–197; see 195.

14. Danto, "Beauty for Ashes," 195.

15. See, for instance, Stephen Westfall's article, "Slow Painting," *Art in America* 12 (February 2018): 62–67, which claims, by way of a subtitle, that "The Deliberate Pace at Which a Painting Demands to Be Viewed Is Key to Its Contemporary Relevance."

16. See here Emmanuel Alloa, *La résistance du sensible: Merleau-Ponty crititque de la transparence* (Paris: Kimé, 2008).

17. See here Maria Müller Schareck, "'Out Into the World': How Agnes Martin's Paintings Reached Germany and Western Europe," in *Agnes Martin*, ed. Frances Morris and Tiffany Bell (London: Tate, 2015), 205.

18. See Siri Hustvedt, "Giorgio Morandi: Not Just Bottles," in *Mysteries of the Rectangle: Essays on Painting* (New York: Princeton Architectural Press, 2007), 121–134. Li Fangying (1696–1755), whose paintings did not cultivate verisimilitude, is counted among "The Eight Eccentrics of Yangzhou."

19. Danto, "Beauty for Ashes," 195.

20. See Merleau-Ponty's comments on Whitehead in *Nature*, 113–122.

21. N, 186–189. See also Henri Maldiney, *Tal Coat, Regard, Parole, Espace*, ed. Christian Chaput, Philippe Grosos, and Maria Villela-Petit (Paris: Cerf, 2013), 53–60, and 167–174. Tal Coat is the pseudonym of the painter Pierre Louis Jacob (1905–1985).

22. "Denn das Schöne ist nichts / als des Schrecklichen Anfang" (For the beautiful is nothing / but the beginning of the terrible) verses 5 and 6 of *Erste Duineser Elegie*.

23. Cheng, *Fünf Meditationen*, 30.

24. N, 186–189.

25. Although this aspect of Portmann's reasoning in the second (1060) edition of *Die Tiergestalt* has already been mentioned in this book, its importance needs to be emphasized. Since unaddressed appearances are not geared even to mate choice based on aesthetic pleasure (as to which see the discussion of Richard Prum's work in the introduction to this book, "A Plethora of Issues"), they seem to attest to the possibility of aesthetic creativity in nature divorced entirely from function.

26. Maldiney, *Tal Coat*, 56. The essay dates from 1954.

27. OE, 87; EM, 376.

28. See here François Berthier's discussion in *Reading Zen in the Rocks*, translated, edited, and with a philosophical essay by Graham Parkes (Chicago: University of Chicago Press, 2000). It is remarkable that, as Berthier brings to the reader's attention, this iconic work was created in a time of famine and civil war, as well as by laborers considered to be subhuman. Echoing Merleau-Ponty's emphasis on an artwork's hermeneutic fecundity, to Berthier also "every masterpiece is inexhaustible" (76).

29. Chrétien, "Introduction," in *Regard, Parole, Espace* by Henri Maldiney (Paris: Les Editions du Cerf, 2013), 29.

30. Danto, "Beauty for Ashes," 183–184.

31. See Cézanne to Emile Bernard, October 23, 1905, Michael Doran, ed., *Conversations with Cézanne*, trans. Julie L. Cochran (Berkeley: University of California Press, 2001), 148.

32. Merleau-Ponty, "Cézanne's Doubt," 16.

33. Maldiney, "Tal Coat: Solitude de l'universel," in *Regard, Parole, Espace*, ed. C.Chaput, Ph. Grosos, and M. Villela-Petit, and with a Preface by Jean-Louis Chrétien (Paris: Editions du Cerf, 2013), 171. The essay dates from 1965.

34. Agnes Martin, "Selected Writings," in *Agnes Martin: The Awareness of Perfection*, ed. Barbara Haskell (New York: Harry N. Abrams, 1992), 10.

35. Martin, "Selected Writings," 13, 26.

36. Tiffany Bell, "Happiness Is the Goal," in *Agnes Martin*, ed. Frances Morris and Tiffany Bell (London: Tate, 2015), 27.

37. Haskell, "Agnes Martin: The Awareness of Perfection," 93–118.

38. Rosalind Krauss, "The/Cloud/," in *Agnes Martin: The Awareness of Perfection*, ed. Barbara Haskell (New York: Harry N. Abrams, 1992), 155–165. Krauss's reference is to Kasha Linville, "Agnes Martin: An Appreciation," *Artforum* 9 (June 1971): 72.

39. There is here an evident connection to Jacques Derrida's notion of the supplement as both marginalized and essential.

40. Hubert Damisch, *Théorie de l'image* (Paris: Seuil, 1972).

41. Krauss, "The/Cloud/," 164.

42. Krauss, "The/Cloud/," 164.

43. *Spectrum Colors Arranged by Chance*, I, 1951. Graphite and collage on paper, 19.5 × 39 in. Philadelphia Museum of Art.

44. OE, 43; EM, 362.

45. See here John Gage, *Color and Meaning: Art, Science, and Symbolism* (Berkeley: University of California Press, 1999), 139.

46. OE, 67; EM, 370.

47. Irving Sandler, "Natvar Bhavsar: Painting and the Reality of Color," in Marius Kwint and Irving Sandler, *Natvar Bhavsar: Poetics of Color* (Milan: Skira, 2008), 43.

48. See Sandler, "Natvar Bhavsar," 38; and Marius Kwint, "Color Immersion: Natvar Bhavsar in Conversation," in Marius Kwint and Irving Sandler, *Natvar Bhavsar: Poetics of Color* (Milan: Skira, 2008), 20.

49. Sandler, "Natvar Bhavsar," 44.
50. Sandler, "Natvar Bhavsar," 47.
51. Chrétien, "Introduction," 29.
52. OE, 69; EM, 370. ALF, 13–14, 37.
53. OE, 32; EM, 359.
54. ALF, 56.
55. OE, 32; EM, 359.
56. OE, 32; EM, 359.
57. IP, 38.
60. IP, 179. See here Sanja Delanovic, "Through the Fold: A Jointure of Gilles Deleuze and Jean-Luc Nancy," *Philosophy Today* 60, no. 2 (Spring 2016): 325–345. Delanovic writes: "[The] manner in which Nancy articulates the event as a kind of restlessness [is] best encapsulated by the verb to be born, to never cease being born . . ." (330). On memory and anteriority to the subjective dimension, see also Robert Vallier, "Memory—of the Future: Institution and Memory in the Later Merleau-Ponty," in *Time, Memory, Institution: Merleau-Ponty's New Ontology of Self*, ed. David Morris and Kym McLaren (Athens: Ohio University Press, 2015), 109–129.

61. Heidegger, *Holzwege*, 53.

62. Merleau-Ponty, "Problematic of the Visible and the Invisible," Working Note of January 1960, VI, 282; 229.

63. Anna Caterina Dalmasso, "L'artiste et l'adversité: hazard et création chez Merleau-Ponty," *Chiasmi* 17 (2015): 201–222.

64. Michael McCanne, "New Museum Triennial," exhibition review of *Songs for Sabotage* at the New Museum, New York, *Art in America* (May–June 2018): https://www.artinamericamagazine.com/reviews/new-museum-triennial-2/.

Conclusion

1. See VI, chapter 3, "Interrogation and Intuition."
2. Jacobus, *Reading Cy Twombly*, 234–235.
3. It would also be interesting to consider the role of hyperrealism in the context of the art of Vija Celmins, from her early images of such mundane things as erasers to her haunting oceanic or lunar images.
4. Stephen Westfall, "Slow Painting," *Art in America* 12 (February 2018): 62–69.
5. Westfall, "Slow Painting," 64.
6. Westfall, "Slow Painting," 65.

Selected Bibliography

Works and Editions of Works by Merleau-Ponty

Merleau-Ponty, Maurice. *Causeries, 1948*. Paris: Seuil, 2002.
———. "Cézanne's Doubt." In *Sense and Non-Sense*, translated by Hubert L. Dreyfus and Patricia Allen Dreyfus. Evanston: Northwestern University Press, 1991.
———. "Faith and Good Faith." In *Sense and Non-Sense*, translated by Hubert L. Dreyfus and Patricia Allen Dreyfus. Evanston: Northwestern University Press, 1964.
———. "In Praise of Philosophy." In *In Praise of Philosophy and Other Essays*, edited by John Wild and James Edie, and translated by John O'Neill. Evanston: Northwestern University Press, 1988.
———. "L'homme et l'adversité." In *Signes*. Paris: Gallimard, 1960.
———. *L'institution dans l'histoire personnelle et publique: Le problème de la passivité, le sommeil, l'inconscient, la mémoire: Notes de cours au Collège de France*. Paris: Éditions Belin, 2003.
———. "Le langage indirect et les voix du silence." In *Signes*. Paris: Gallimard, 1960.
———. "Man and Adversity," translated by Richard C. McCleary. In *Signs*. Evanston: Northwestern University Press, 1964.
———. *Merleau-Ponty: Texts and Dialogues*. Edited by Hugh J. Silverman and James Barry Jr. Atlantic Highlands: Humanities Press, 1992.
———. *The Merleau-Ponty Aesthetics Reader: Philosophy and Painting*. Edited by Galen A. Johnson and Michael B. Smith. Evanston: Northwestern University Press, 1993.
———. *The Merleau-Ponty Reader*. Edited by Ted Toadvine and Leonard Lawlor. Evanston: Northwestern University Press, 2007.
———. *La nature: Notes de cours du Collège de France*. Paris: Seuil, 1995.
———. *Nature: Course Notes from the Collège de France*. Translated by Robert Vallier, and edited and with notes by Dominique Séglard, III. Evanston: Northwestern University Press, 2003.

———. *Notes de cours, 1959–1961*. Edited by Stéphanie Ménasé. Paris: Gallimard, 1996.
———. *Notes de cours sur l'origine de la géométrie de Husserl, suivi de recherches sur la phénoménologie de Merleau-Ponty*. Edited by Renaud Barbaras. Paris: Presses Universitaires de France, 1998.
———. *L'œil et l'esprit*. Paris: Gallimard, 1964.
———. *Phénoménologie de la perception*. Paris: Gallimard, 1945.
———. *Phenomenology of Perception*. Translated by Donald A. Landes. London: Routledge, 2012.
———. *Le primat de la perception et ses conséquences philosophiques*. Grenoble: Cynara, 1964.
———. *The Primacy of Perception*. Edited and translated by James M. Edie. Evanston: Northwestern University Press, 1989.
———. *The Prose of the World*. Edited by Claude Lefort and translated by John O'Neill. Evanston: Northwestern University Press, 1991.
———. *Sens et non-sense*. 3rd rev. ed. Paris: Nagel, 1961.
———. *Sense and Non-Sense*. Translated by Hubert L. Dreyfus and Patricia Allen Dreyfus. Evanston: Northwestern University Press, 1991.
———. *Signes*. Paris: Gallimard, 1960.
———. *Signs*. Translated by Richard C. McCleary. Evanston: Northwestern University Press, 1964.
———. *The Structure of Behavior*. Translated by Alden L. Fisher. Pittsburgh: Duquesne University Press, 2008.
———. *Le visible et l'invisible, suivi de notes de travail*. Edited by Claude Lefort. Paris: Gallimard, 1964.
———. *The Visible and the Invisible, Followed by Working Notes*. Edited by Claude Lefort and translated by Alphonso Lingis. Evanston: Northwestern University Press, 1968.
———. *The World of Perception*. Translated by Oliver Davis. London: Routledge, 2004.

Works or Collections of Works on Merleau-Ponty

Alloa, Emmanuel. *La résistance du sensible: Merleau-Ponty, critique de la transparence*. Paris: Kimé, 2008.
Alloa, Emmanuel, and Adnen Jdey, eds. *Du sensible á l'œuvre: Esthétiques de Merleau-Ponty*. Brussels: La lettre volée, 2012.
Barbaras, Renaud. "L'autonomie de l'apparaître." *Chiasmi* 15 (2014): 27–35.
———. *The Being of the Phenomenon: Merleau-Ponty's Ontology*. Translated by Ted Toadvine and Richard Lawlor. Bloomington: Indiana University Press, 2004.
———. *Le tournant de l'expérience: Recherches sur la philosophie de Merleau-Ponty*. Paris: Vrin, 1998.

Barthes, Roland. "Cy Twombly ou 'Non multa sed multum.'" In *Cy Twombly: Cinquante années de dessin*, edited by Jonas Storsve and Simon Schama, 37–42. Paris: Éditions Gallimard / Centre Pompidou, 2004.

———. *The Responsibility of Forms: Critical Essays on Music, Art, and Representation*. Translated by Richard Howard. New York: Hill and Wang, 1985.

Carbone, Mauro. *The Flesh of Images: Merleau-Ponty between Painting and Cinema*. Translated by Marta Nijhuis. Albany: State University of New York Press, 2015.

———. *The Thinking of the Sensible: Merleau-Ponty's A-Philosophy*. Evanston: Northwestern University Press, 2005.

Dalmasso, Anna Caterina. *Le corps, c'est l'écran: La philosophie du visuel de Merleau-Ponty*. Paris: Éditions Mimésis, 2018.

Delanovicz, Sanja. "Through the Fold: A Jointure of Gilles Deleuze and Jean-Luc Nancy." *Philosophy Today* 60 (Spring 2016): 325–345.

Flynn, Bernard, Wayne J. Froman, and Robert Vallier, eds. *Merleau-Ponty and the Possibilities of Philosophy*. Albany: State University of New York Press, 2007.

Fóti, Véronique M. *Tracing Expression in Merleau-Ponty: Aesthetics, Philosophy of Biology, and Ontology*. Evanston: Northwestern University Press, 2013.

Johnson, Galen A. *The Retrieval of the Beautiful: Thinking Through Merleau-Ponty's Aesthetics*. Evanston: Northwestern University Press, 2010.

Kaushik, Rajiv. *Art and Institution: Aesthetics in the Late Works of Merleau-Ponty*. London: Continuum, 2011.

———. *Art, Language and Figure in Merleau-Ponty: Excursions in Hyper-Dialectic*. London: Bloomsbury, 2013.

———. "The Shape of Things: Separation and Symbolics in Merleau-Ponty." *Chiasmi* 18 (2016): 313–330.

Ménasé, Stéphanie. *Passivité et création: Merleau-Ponty et l'art moderne*. Paris: Presses Universitaires de France, 2003.

Morris, David. *Merleau-Ponty's Developmental Ontology*. Evanston: Northwestern University Press, 2018.

Morris, David, and Kym McLaren, eds. *Time, Memory, Institution: Merleau-Ponty's New Ontology of Self*. Athens: Ohio University Press, 2015.

Neuenschwander, Simone, and Thomas Thiel, eds. *Transparenzen / Transparencies: Zur Ambivalenz einer neuen Sichtbarkeit*. Nuremberg: Bielefelder Kunstverein and Sternberg Press, 2016.

Saint-Aubert, Emmanuel de. "Conscience et expression chez Merleau-Ponty." *Chiasmi* 10 (2008): 85–106.

Silverman, Hugh J., and James Barry Jr., eds. *Texts and Dialogues: Merleau-Ponty*. Atlantic Highlands: Humanities Press, 1992.

Toadvine, Ted. *Merleau-Ponty's Philosophy of Nature*. Evanston: Northwestern University Press, 2009.

Vallier, Robert. "The Indiscernible Joining: Structure, Signification, and Animality in Merleau-Ponty's *La nature*." *Chiasmi* 3 (2001): 187–212.

———. "Memory—of the Future Institution and Memory in the Later Merleau-Ponty." In *Time, Memory, Institution: Merleau-Ponty's New Ontology of Self*, ed. David Morris and Kym McLaren, 109–129. Athens: Ohio University Press, 2015.

Waldenfels, Bernhard. "Going and Coming of Time." In *Time, Memory, Institution: Merleau-Ponty's New Ontology of Self*, edited by David Morris and Kym McLaren, 217–237. Athens: Ohio University Press.

Other Philosophical Works

Benso, Silvia. *Pensare Doppo Auschwitz: Etica Filosofica e Teodicea Ebraica*. Naples: Edizione Scientifiche Italiane, 1992.

Berthier, François. *Reading Zen in the Rocks: The Japanese Dry Landscape Garden*. Translated, edited, and with a philosophical essay by Graham Parkes. Chicago: University of Chicago Press, 2000.

Cheng, François. *Fünf Meditationen über die Schönheit*. Translated by Judith Klein. Munich: C. H. Beck, 2008.

———. *Vide et plein: Le langage pictoral chinois*. Paris: Seuil, 1991.

Derrida, Jacques. *Cinders*. Edited and translated by Ned Lukacher. Lincoln: University of Nebraska Press, 1987.

———. *Memoirs of the Blind: The Self-Portrait and Other Ruins*. Translated by Pascale-Anne Brault and Michael Naas. Chicago: University of Chicago Press, 1993.

Fóti, Véronique M. "Adversity and Practices of Painting: Merleau-Ponty, Monet, and Joan Mitchell." *Philosophy Today* 60, no. 2 (Spring 2016): 397–406.

———. *Epochal Discordance: Hölderlin's Philosophy of Tragedy*. Albany: State University of New York Press, 2006.

———. *Heidegger and the Poets: Poiēsis/Sophia/Technē*. Atlantic Highlands: Humanities Press, 1992.

———. *Vision's Invisibles: Philosophical Explorations*. Albany: State University of New York Press, 2003.

Freud, Sigmund. *Standard Edition of the Complete Psychological Works of Sigmund Freud*. London: Hogarth Press, 1954–1975.

Heidegger, Martin. *Besinnung*. Edited by Friedrich-Wilhelm von Herrmann, *Gesamtausgabe*, 66. Frankfurt am Main: Vittorio Klostermann, 1997.

———. "Das Ding." In *Vorträge und Aufsätze*, vol. 2, 3rd ed. Pfullingen: Neske, 1967.

———. *Die Grundbegriffe der Metaphysik: Welt–Endlichkeit–Einsamkeit*. Edited by Friedrich-Wilhelm von Herrmann, *Gesamtausgabe*, 29–30. Frankfurt am Main: Vittorio Klostermann, 1983.

———. *Holzwege*. *Gesamtausgabe*, 5, 2nd ed. Edited by Friedrich-Wilhelm von Herrmann. Frankfurt am Main: Vittorio Klostermann,1977.

———. "Der Ursprung des Kunstwerkes." In *Holzwege*, 4th ed. Frankfurt am Main: Vittorio Klostermann, 1963.
———. *Vorträge und Aufsätze*, 2nd ed. Edited by Friedrich-Wilhelm von Herrmann. *Gesamtausgabe*, 7. Frankfurt am Main: Vittorio Klostermann, 1962.
Homolka, Walter, and Arnulf Heidegger, eds. *Heidegger und der Antisemitismus: Positionen im Widerstreit: Mit Briefen von Martin und Fritz Heidegger*. Freiburg: Herder, 2016.
Nancy, Jean-Luc. *The Ground of the Image*. Translated by Jeff Fort. New York: Fordham University Press, 2001.
———. *The Muses*. Translated by Peggy Kamuf. Stanford: Stanford University Press, 1996.
Russon, John. *Sites of Exposure: Art, Politics, and the Nature of Experience*. Bloomington: Indiana University Press, 2017.
Schmidt, Dennis J. "'Like a fire that consumes all before it': On Language and Image." *Lyrical and Ethical Subjects: Essays on the Periphery of the Word, Freedom, and History*, 141–162. Albany: State University Press, 2005.
Schmitz, Hermann. "Heidegger und der Nationalsozialismus." In *Heidegger und der Antisemismus: Positionen im Widerstreit: Mit Briefen von Martin und Fritz Heidegger*, edited by Walter Homolka and Arnulf Heidegger, 326–341. Freiburg: Herder, 2016.
Serres, Michel. *Malfeasance*. Translated by Anne-Marie Feenberg-Dibon. Stanford: Stanford University Press, 2011.
Taminiaux, Jacques. "The Origin of 'The Origin of the Work of Art.'" In *Poetics, Speculation, and Judgment: The Shadow of the Work of Art from Kant to Phenomenology*, edited and translated by Michael Gendre, 153–169. Albany: State University of New York Press, 1993.
Tanke, Joseph J. *Jacques Rancière, an Introduction: Philosophy, Politics, Aesthetics*. London: Continuum, 2011.

Art and Artists

Aagesen, Dorthe, and Rebecca Rabinow, eds. *Matisse: In Search of True Painting*. New York: The Metropolitan Museum of Art, 2012.
Abramovicz, Janet. *Giorgio Morandi: The Art of Silence*. New Haven: Yale University Press, 2004.
Albers, Patricia. *Joan Mitchell, Lady Painter: A Life*. New York: Knopf, 2011.
Amory, Dita, ed. *Madame Cézanne*. New York: The Metropolitan Museum of Art, 2014.
Ashton, Dore. Catalogue essay. In *Milton Avery: Mexico*. New York: Grace Borgenicht Gallery, 1983.

Axsom, Richard H. *Drawn from Nature: The Plant Lithographs of Ellsworth Kelly.* New Haven: Yale University Press, 2005.
Bandera, Maria Cristina. "Contemporanità di Morandi / Morandi Our Contemporary." In *Giorgio Morandi*, ed. Maria Cristina Bandera and Marco Franciolli, 14–51. Milan: Silvana Editoriale, 2012.
Bandera, Maria Cristina, and Marco Franciolli, eds. *Giorgio Morandi*. Milan: Silvana Editoriale, 2012.
Beaumelle, Agnès de la, ed. *Henri Matisse—Ellsworth Kelly: Dessins de Plantes*. Paris: Gallimard/Centre Pompidou, 2002.
Bell, Tiffany. "Happiness Is the Goal." In *Agnes Martin*, edited by Frances Morris and Tiffany Bell, 18–53. London: Tate, 2015.
Benezra, Neal, and Olga M. Viso. *Regarding Beauty: A View of the Late Twentieth Century*. Washington, DC: Hirshhorn Museum and Sculpture Garden, with Hatje Cantz Publishers, 1999.
Bernstock, Judith E. *Joan Mitchell*. New York: Hudson Hill Press, 1988.
Bonnefoy, Françoise, ed. *Joan Mitchell*. Paris: Éditions du Jeu de Paume, 1994.
Bowles, Frances, ed. *No Limits: Zao Wou-Ki*. New York: Asia Society, 2012.
Breslin, James. *Mark Rothko: A Biography*. Chicago: University of Chicago Press, 1993.
"Brice Marden and Chris Ofili in Conversation." *Art Forum International* (October 2006).
Cassar, Jacques. *Dossier Camille Claudel*. Preface by Jeanne Fayard. Paris: Archimbaud-Klincksiek, 2011.
Cheim, John. *Joan Mitchell: An Exhibition of Paintings from October 25 to November 25, 1989, at the Robert Miller Gallery, New York*. Exhibition catalogue, 1989.
Cullinan, Nicholas. "American-Type Painting." In *Cy Twombly: Cycles and Seasons*, edited by Nicholas Serota, 64–69. London: Tate, 2008.
———. "Mourning and Melancholia: *Nini's Paintings*." In *Cy Twombly: Cycles and Seasons*, edited by Nicholas Serota, 136–149. London: Tate, 2008.
Damisch, Hubert. *Théorie de l'image*. Paris: Seuil, 1972.
Danto, Arthur C. "Beauty for Ashes." In *Regarding Beauty: A View of the Late Twentieth Century*, ed. Neal Benezra and Olga M. Viso, 183–197. Washington, DC: Hirshhorn Museum and Sculpture Garden, with Hatje Cantz Publishers, 1999.
Dean, Tacita. "A Panegyric." In *Cy Twombly: Cycles and Seasons*, edited by Nicholas Serota, 32–41. London: Tate, 2008.
de Chassey, Eric. "Aller avec . . ." In *Henri Matisse—Ellsworth Kelly: Dessins de Plantes*. Paris: Gallimard/Centre Pompidou, 2002.
Delahunty, Gavin. "Memory Recorded and Transferred." In Tricia Y. Paik, *Ellsworth Kelly*. London: Phaidon, 2015.
Doran, Michael, ed. *Conversations with Cézanne*. Translated by Julie L. Cochran. Berkeley: University of California Press, 2001.

Engberg, Siri, ed. *Kiki Smith: A Gathering, 1980–2005, with Contributions by Linda Nochlin, Lynne Tillman, and Marina Warner*. Minneapolis: Walker Arts Center, 2006.
Fóti, Véronique M. "Adversity and Practices of Painting: Merleau-Ponty, Monet, and Joan Mitchell." *Philosophy Today* 60, no. 2 (2016): 397–406.
Frankel, David, ed. *Plane Image: A Brice Marden Retrospective*. New York: Museum of Modern Art, 2006.
Gage, John. *Color and Meaning: Art, Science, and Symbolism*. Berkeley: University of California Press, 1999.
Garrels, Gary. "Painting and Architecture." In Tricia Y. Paik, *Ellsworth Kelly*. London: Phaidon, 2015.
Garrels, Gary, ed. *Vija Celmins: To Fix the Image in Memory*. New Haven: Yale University Press, in conjunction with San Francisco Museum of Modern Art, n.d.
Gowrie, Grey, Jooles Holland, Richard Demarco, Martyn Rix, and Shirley Sherwood. *Rory McEwen: The Colors of Reality*, rev. ed. Woodbridge, Suffolk: Royal Botanic Gardens, 2015.
Gribaldo, Paula, ed. *Natvar Bhavsar: Poetics of Color*. Milan: Skira, 2008.
Hacklin, Saara. *Divergences of Perception: The Possibilities of Merleau-Pontian Phenomenology in Analyses of Contemporary Art*. Helsinki: University of Helsinki Press, 2012.
Haskell, Barbara, ed. *Agnes Martin: The Awareness of Perfection*. New York: Whitney Museum of American Art, 1991.
Hass, Nancy. "Enchanted: In Her Four-Decade Career the Artist Kiki Smith Has Created a Visual Iconography . . ." *New York Times Style Magazine*, December 2, 2008, 153–157.
Hustvedt, Siri. "The Drama of Perception: Looking at Morandi." In *Giorgio Morandi*, edited by Maria Cristina Bandera and Marco Franciolli, 254–269. Milan: Silvana Editoriale, 2012.
———. *Mysteries of the Rectangle: Essays on Painting*. Hudson: Princeton Architectural Press, 2006.
———. "Vermeer's Annunciation." In *Mysteries of the Rectangle: Essays on Painting*. Hudson: Princeton Architectural Press, 2006.
Jacobus, Mary. *Reading Cy Twombly: Poetry in Painting*. Princeton: Princeton University Press, 2016.
Kalina, Richard. "The Here and Then: A Cy Twombly Retrospective in Paris Reveals the Artist's Lifelong Fascination with Personal and Historical Memory." *Art in America*, April 2017, 72–81.
Kelly, Ellsworth. "Notes of 1969." In *Theories and Documents of Contemporary Art: A Sourcebook of Artists' Writings*, edited by Kristine Stiles and Peter Selz, 2nd rev. and expanded edition by Kristine Selz, 92–93. Berkeley: University of California Press, 2012.

Kertess, Klaus. *Brice Marden: Paintings and Drawings.* New York: Harry N. Abrams, 1992.

———. *Joan Mitchell.* New York: Harry N. Abrams, 1997.

Kress, W. John, and Shirley Sherwood. *The Art of Plant Evolution.* Woodbridge, Suffolk: Royal Botanic Gardens, 2009.

Kwint, Marius. "Color Immersion: Natvar Bhavsar in Conversation." In *Natvar Bhavsar: Poetics of Color*, edited by Paula Gribaldo, 9–26. Milan: Skira, 2008.

Labrusse, Rémi. "Le désir de la ligne." In *Henri Matisse—Ellsworth Kelly: Dessins de Plantes.* Paris: Gallimard/Centre Pompidou, 2002.

Lewison, Jeremy. *Turner, Monet, Twombly: Later Paintings.* London: Tate, 2012.

Lippard, Lucy. *Eva Hesse.* New York: Da Capo Press, 1976.

Livingston, Jane. "The Paintings of Joan Mitchell." In *The Paintings of Joan Mitchell*, edited by Jane Livingston, with essays by Linda Nochlin, Yvetter Y. Lee, and Jane Livingston. Berkeley: University of California Press, 2002.

Livingston, Jane, ed. *The Paintings of Joan Mitchell.* With Essays by Linda Nochlin, Yvetter Y. Lee, and Jane Livingston. Berkeley: University of California Press, 2002.

"Lynne Tillman in Conversation with Kiki Smith, New York, Sept. 9, 2004." In *Kiki Smith: A Gathering, 1980–2005*, edited by Siri Engberg. Minneapolis: Walker Art Center, 2006.

Lyon, Christopher. "Free Fall: Kiki Smith on Her Art." In Helaine Posner, *Kiki Smith.* New York: The Monacelli Press, 2012.

Maldiney, Henri. *Tal Coat: Regard, Parole, Espace.* Edited by Christian Chaput, Philippe Grosos, and Maria Villela-Petit. Paris: Cerf, 2013.

Martin, Agnes. "Selected Writings." In *Agnes Martin: The Awareness of Perfection*, edited by Barbara Haskell. New York: Harry N. Abrams, 1992.

McBreen, Ellen, and Helen Burnham. *Matisse in the Studio.* Boston: Museum of Fine Arts, 1917.

Mee, Margaret. *Amazon: Diaries of an Artist Explorer.* Woodbridge, Suffolk: Antique Collectors Club and Royal Botanic Gardens, Kew, 2004.

Michaud, Yves. "Entretiens." In *Joan Mitchell*, edited by Françoise Bonnefoy, 23–32. Paris: Réunion des Musées Nationaux, 1994.

Miller, M. H. "A Temple for Light." *New York Times Style Magazine*, February 18, 2018, 218–223.

Morris, Frances, and Tiffany Bell, eds. *Agnes Martin.* London: Tate, 2015.

Nancy, Jean-Luc. The Ground of the Image. Trans. Jeff Fort. New York: Fordham University Press, 2005.

Nochlin, Linda. "Joan Mitchell: A Rage to Paint." In *The Paintings of Joan Mitchell*, ed. Jane Livingston. Berkeley: University of California Press, 2002.

Paik, Tricia Y. *Ellsworth Kelly.* With contributions from Gavin Delahunty, Gary Garrells, Richard Schiff, and Robert Storr. London: Phaidon, 2015.

Pavlouskova, Nela. *Cy Twombly: Late Paintings, 2003–2011.* Translated by David H. Wilson. London: Thames and Hudson, 2015.

Posner, Helaine. *Kiki Smith*. New York: The Monacelli Press, 2005.
Pratber, Marla, and Michael Senff, eds. *Ellsworth Kelly: Plant Drawings, 1948–2010*. Munich: Schirmer Mosel Verlag, 2015.
Rivkin, Joshua. *Chalk: The Art and Erasure of Cy Twombly*. New York: Melville House, 2018.
Sandler, Irving. "Natvar Bhavsar: Painting and the Reality of Color." In *Natvar Bhavsar: Poetics of Color*, edited by Paula Gribaldo, 27–48. Milan: Skira, 2008.
Serota, Nicholas, ed. *Cy Twombly: Cycles and Seasons*. London: Tate, 2008.
Sherwood, Shirley. *Contemporary Botanical Artists: The Shirley Sherwood Collection*. New York: Cross River Press, 1919.
———. *A Passion for Plants: Contemporary Botanical Masterworks*. London: Weidenfeld and Nicholson, 2003.
Stiles, Kristina, and Peter Selz, eds. *Theories and Documents of Contemporary Art: A Sourcebook of Artists' Writings*. 2nd rev. and expanded edition by Kristina Selz. New Haven: Yale University Press, 2005.
Storr, Robert. "Starting Out—Starting Over." In Tricia Y. Paik, *Ellsworth Kelly*. London: Phaidon Press, 2015.
Storsve, Jonas, and Simon Schama, eds. *Cy Twombly: Cinquante Années de Dessins*. Paris: Éditions Gallimard / Centre Pompidou, 2004.
Sylvester, Julie, and Philip Larratt-Smith, eds. *Cy Twombly: Paradise*. Santa Maria Tuperlac, Mexico: Fundación de Arte Contemporáneo, 2014.
Twombly, Cy, and Nicholas Serota. "History Behind the Thought." In *Cy Twombly: Cycles and Seasons*, edited by Nicholas Serota, 42–53. London: Tate, 2008.
Varnedoe, Kirk. *Cy Twombly: A Retrospective*. New York: Harry N. Abrams, 1994.
———. "Inscriptions in Arcadia." In *Cy Twombly: A Retrospective*. New York: Harry N. Abrams, 1994.
Ventura, Yasmil Raymond, with Max Andrews. "Chronology." In *Kiki Smith: A Gathering, 1980–2005*, edited by Siri Engberg, 54–79. Minneapolis: Walker Arts Center, 2006.
Walt, Melissa, Ankeney Weitz, and Michelle Yun, eds. *No Limits: Zao Wou-Ki*. New York and Waterville: Asia Society and Colby College of Art, 2006.
Warner, Marina. "Wolf-Girl, Soul-Bird: The Mortal Art of Kiki Smith." In *Kiki Smith: A Gathering, 1980–2005*, edited by Siri Engberg, 42–53. Minneapolis: Walker Arts Center, 2006.
Watkins, James, ed. *Cézanne*. Philadelphia: Philadelphia Museum of Art, 1996.
Westfall, Stephen. "Slow Painting." *Art in America*, February 2018, 62–69.

Biology

Dewitte, Jacques. "L'interanimalité comme intercorporéité et intervisibilité: Merleau-Ponty lecteur de Portmann." In *Corps et individuation*, edited by Pierre-François Moreau and Jean Gayon, 89–119. Dijon: Universitaires de Dijon, 1998.

Haskell, David George. *The Forest Unseen: A Year's Watch in Nature*. New York: Viking, 2012.

Karban, Richard. *Plant Sensing and Communication*. Chicago: University of Chicago Press, 2015.

Lewington, Anna. *Ancient Trees: Trees That Live for a Thousand Years*. London: Batsford, 2012.

Marden, Michael. *Plant Thinking: A Philosophy of Vegetal Life*. New York: Columbia University Press, 2013.

Pollan, Michael. "The Intelligent Plant: Scientists Debate a New Way to Understand Flora." *New Yorker*, December 23 and 30, 2013, 92–105.

Portmann, Adolf. *Die Tiergestalt: Studien über die Bedeutung der tierischen Erscheinung*, 2nd rev. ed. Basel: Friedrich Reinhardt, 1960.

Prum, Richard O. *The Evolution of Beauty: How Darwin's Forgotten Theory of Mate Choice Shapes the Animal World—and Us*. New York: Doubleday, 2017.

Tuttle, Merlin. *The Secret Lives of Bats: My Adventures with the World's Most Misunderstood Mammals*. New York: Houghton Mifflin, 2015.

Uexküll, Jakob von. *Umwelt und Innenwelt der Tiere*. Berlin: Springer Verlag, 1909.

Wohlleben, Peter. *The Hidden Life of Trees: What They Feel, How They Communicate*. Translated by Jane Billinghurst. New York: Random House, 2015.

Index of Topics

Abstract Expressionism, 48, 64, 102
Animality, 9, 27, 32, 56, 110
Animals, 10, 28, 32, 34, 89, 98; animal world articulation, 38; inter-animality, 27; inter-being with, 9, 37
Art and art works, 6f, 14f, 33, 49f, 57, 62, 98f, 105; ethical impact of, 6, 11; hermeneutic fecundity of, 54

Beauty, 10f, 34f, 38, 64, 70, 93–100, 102–107; and invisibles, 105; and perfection, 94, 96, 100f; strong, 97f, 1101, 103f
Body, 8, 27f, 31f, 31–36, 38f, 47, 50–53, 55f, 69, 72f, 79, 94–96, 46, 72, 94
Botanical Art, 84–86, 91

Chance, Contingency, 3f, 11, 22, 30f, 34–36, 80, 100–105
Color, 19, 64–71, 102f, 108f

Diacritics, 38, 44, 51, 79
Duality, 4f, 7, 41, 76, 98, 109f

Ecology, 8f, 27, 31f, 41
Effacement, erasure, 48f, 109
Elementarity, 41, 56–59, 70, 110f

Essences, 76f, 107, 110; carnal, 19, 46, 72, 94
Event, 38f, 103–105, 109

Fascism, 20–22, 37, 93
Figuration and abstraction, 4, 7, 13, 19, 72, 75, 84, 99–100, 107, 111
Film, 2, 18, 56
Flesh, 4, 17, 31, 35, 40f, 56–58, 68f, 71, 73

Image, 5, 14, 20, 45, 48f, 48, 51f, 59, 68, 109, 111
Institution, 40, 48, 104–110

Light, 8, 18f, 24f, 59, 62f, 66–68, 70–72, 102, 108–111
Line and Edge, 80–100

Manifestation, 19, 47f, 59, 97, 109
Materiality, 4, 31, 40f, 45, 52, 62–64, 108, 112
Memory, 7, 17f, 21, 40, 50, 63, 78–80, 90; commemoration, 54f
Motion, 17, 55f, 68

Names, 45, 49–54, 109
Nature, 8, 23f–29, 36, 63, 68, 71, 89, 98–103

Painting, 8, 17f, 68–73, 96–98, 100; and architecture, 9, 21, 83f, 109; historicity of, 76f; relation to action and language, 8, 43f, 53f; slow, 111f
Perception, 28, 38
Plant drawing, 9, 75–85, 90f, 102, 110f
Plants, 9, 87–91
Play, 34, 38f, 87f
Poetry, 5, 44f, 48, 51f, 58

Rhythm, 19, 46, 90, 110f

Space, 7f, 17, 19, 57, 66f, 82f, 87, 90
Symbols, signs, 45, 89

Things, thing-being, 6f, 13–26, 62
Time, 90
Trace, 5f, 45, 48, 57f, 110

Vision, 19f, 44, 49; precessions of, 14; "profane," 14, 41, 47, 73; of, 14; relation to invisibles, 41

Whiteness, 32, 57, 66, 68, 72f

Index of Persons

Arcangeli, Francesco, 23f
Audubon, John James, 76, 85
Axsom, Richard H., 79, 86

Bacon, Francis, 32
Barbaras, Renault, 57
Barreau, Gisèle, 69
Barthes, Roland, 44, 47, 51
Basquiat, Jean-Michel, 5
Beckmann, Max, 77
Bergson, Henri, 31
Bernstock, Judith, 65, 67f
Bhavsar, Natvar, 102f
Brunelleschi, Filippo, 100f

Caravaggio, 84f
Carbone, Mauro, 2, 4, 14, 56, 68, 112
Cèzanne, Paul, 1f, 5, 14, 16, 19–21, 63, 66, 70–72, 77, 82, 99f, 105
Cheng, François, 94, 98
Chrótien, Jean-Louis, 98, 104
Coghill, George E., 87
Cullinan, Nicholas, 46–48, 50f, 54, 58

Dalmasso, Anna Caterina, 2, 105
Damisch, Hubert, 100
Danto, Arthur, 95, 95f, 99
Darwin, Charles Robert, 10
Da Vinci, Leonardo, 44, 47, 85f

Dean, Tacita, 48, 57
De Kooning, Willem, 64, 95
De la Tour, Georges, 67
Derrida, Jacques, 48
Descartes, René, 17, 44, 67f, 72, 77–80, 83, 91, 98, 102
Duchamp, Marcel, 96

El Greco (Domenikos Theotokopoulos), 108
Eliot, Thomas Stearns, 44f, 58, 61

Freud, Lucian, 95, 99

Greenberg, Clement, 63, 102
Gonzalez-Torres, Felix, 99
Goya y Lucientes, Francisco de, 32, 95f

Haskell, David George, 38
Heidegger, Martin, 4, 6–9, 13–16, 25f, 35–38, 49, 68, 70, 72, 76, 89, 91, 94, 97, 105, 108; beauty/truth, 35, 37; Fourfold, 7, 15f; things of use, 36f
Hesse, Eva, 40, 99
Hölderlin, Friedrich, 50f
Homer, 50, 53–55, 73
Husserl, Edmund, 73
Hustvedt, Siri, 14, 18, 20

151

Index of Persons

Jacobus, Mary, 45f, 51–56, 107
Johnson, Galen A., 2, 38f, 94

Kant, Emmanuel, 38, 103
Kaushik, Rajiv, 2, 44f, 51, 58, 104
Kearney, Richard, 38
Kelly, Ellsworth, 3f, 8f, 11, 13, 75–91, 101f, 108–111; and architecture, 9f, 80, 83f; plant drawings and lithographs, 79, 83f, 86, 90, 102, 110f; sculpture, 82f; spectrum, 80f, 102, 109
Kertess, Klaus, 63f, 66, 70
Klee, Paul, 1–5, 14, 44–46, 61, 84, 86, 95f, 111
Kline, Franz, 64, 66
Krauss, Rosalind, 100–103

Li, Fangying, 96
Lyotard, François, 38
Locke, Patricia, 88

Maldiney, Henri, 97f, 100, 104
Mallarmé, Stéphane, 44
Marden, Brice, 99
Martin, Agnes, 11, 64, 95, 99–103
Matisse, Henri, 1f, 18, 63, 67, 71, 76, 84, 86, 94–96, 107–110
McEwen, Rory, 85–87, 110
Merleau-Ponty, Maurice, 1–11, 13–26, 33–39, 43–51, 56–69, 75, 84–98, 105–112; animality, 27–35; elementality, flesh, 41, 56f, 65–69; Incarnation, 31, 94; institution, 40; non-positivity of presencing, 7, 101; painting, 8, 43, 51, 53f, 65–69, 79, 102f
Michaud, Yves, 45, 62, 65f, 71, 98
Mitchell, Joan, 3, 7–11, 46, 61–73, 105, 107–109; *La Grande Vallée*, 69–72; painting's elision of language, 61

Mondrian, Piet, 16, 102
Monet, Claude, 21, 57, 63, 67, 105
Moore, Henry, 97
Morandi, Giorgio, 3f, 7, 13–26; and fascism, 20–22, 95f, 107f; late still lifes and landscapes, 21–24
Morris, David, 2f, 26

Nancy, Jean-Luc, 93f
Newman, Barnett, 2, 95
Newton, Isaac, 102
Nietzsche, Friedrich, 52
Nochlin, Linda, 32, 63, 67

O'Hara, Frank, 61, 66, 68

Paz, Octavio, 44, 58f
Picasso, Pablo, 18, 77, 95f
Plato, 14f, 50f, 54, 64, 67, 69, 100, 110
Pollan, Michael, 90
Portmann, Adolf, 10, 28, 32, 34, 38, 98
Proust, Marcel, 40, 72
Prum, Richard O., 10

Raphael, 51 (Raffaelo Sanzio)
Rilke, Rainer Maria, 44, 57f, 61, 97
Rivkin, Joshua, 53
Rodin, Auguste, 55, 94f

Sartre, Paul, 73
Schmitz, Hermann, 37
Simon, Claude, 61f, 69
Smith, Kiki, 3, 8–12, 27–41 95, 99; Catholicism, 31; creative inspiration, 27, 36, 40; creative inspiration, human and animal bodies, 27–40, 106, 108, 110; Noah's ark, 31f

Taminiaux, Jacques, 15

Tillman, Lynne, 34, 36, 38f
Tobey, Mark, 5, 45
Twombly, Cy, 2–4, 44–58, 95, 101, 107, 109f; erasure, effacement, 48; *Nini's Pintings*, 46f; pictorial writing, 46; poetry, 48; war, 53–57

Uexküll, Jakob von, 9, 37, 38, 89

Valéry, Paul, 46, 72
Van Gogh, Vincent, 36f, 63, 65, 71, 105
Varnedoe, Kirk, 44, 46, 53

Waldenfels, Bernhard, 89
Westfall, Stephe, 11f
Whitehead, Alfred North, 89f, 97

www.ingramcontent.com/pod-product-compliance
Ingram Content Group UK Ltd.
Pitfield, Milton Keynes, MK11 3LW, UK
UKHW041919140426
5217IPUK00013B/236